KARATE
LEGACY
AND
THE POWER
WITHIN

Marie Antonette Gonzalez Waite

To Josette

Just remember

every dreams of yours

put it in yours ♡

Love us

RK Gonzalez

Editing by Faizan Ahmad CH with QA Solutions
Layouts and cover by Fire-Up Media Studio
Published By Fire-Up Connect

COPYRIGHT 2024 All rights reserved.

ISBN: 9798340135957

To my grandfather, Latino Gonzalez, who pioneered Karate in the Philippines and authored *The Techniques of Okinawa Shorin-Ryu Karate.*

To my uncle, Roberto Gonzalez, whose lifelong dedication to Karate brought over 100 movies to life and produced the seminal *Karate Complete.*

To my father, Rolando Gonzalez, a beacon of leadership and protection for our family and community, whose inspiration knew no bounds.

And to my mother, Patricia Gonzalez, a fearless woman who conquers every challenge with grace, sharing her boundless love and care with family, friends, and everyone she meets.

Message From The Editor

C ollaborating with Marie Waite on this book has been a
profoundly enriching experience, touching every
aspect of my life as an editor. As I delved into the
intricacies of the manuscript, I found myself not only
refining my editing skills but also discovering a deeper
connection to the world of martial arts, a theme woven
throughout the narrative.

My experience working with Marie has been nothing
short of inspiring. Her unwavering dedication to her craft
and her genuine appreciation for people from all walks of
life have not only enriched our project but also left a
profound impact on my approach to editing. Together, we
navigated the complexities of storytelling with grace and
precision, each word carefully chosen to convey the
essence of Marie's message.

Through Marie's words, I was transported into the world
of karate, where discipline, resilience, and determination
reign supreme. As an editor, this journey allowed me to
draw parallels between the principles of martial arts and the
art of editing. Just as karate practitioners hone their skills
through rigorous training and unwavering focus, I too
refined my craft with dedication and precision, ensuring
that every word resonated with clarity and purpose.

But beyond the technical aspects of editing, this
collaboration with Marie underscored the power of

storytelling to inspire and uplift, much like the lessons imparted in the dojo. Through her words, I witnessed the transformative impact of karate on individuals' lives, instilling them with confidence, courage, and a sense of purpose. This realization fueled my own commitment to crafting narratives that not only entertain but also empower and enlighten.

This book has been more than just a project; it has been a journey of self-discovery and growth. Through Marie's narrative, I've not only refined my editing skills but also deepened my appreciation for the transformative power of storytelling and the enduring lessons of martial arts. As I turn the final page, I do so with a renewed sense of purpose and gratitude for the opportunity to be part of such a meaningful endeavor.

Faizan Ahmad Ch

Foreword

Reflecting on where I am in life, and thinking of the influential people who have guided me in decision-making and shaping my relationships, I am reminded of my family and its roots. Taking a moment to contemplate the incredible journey of my family, the Gonzalez family, I am overcome with a sense of awe and gratitude. My family's story is one that epitomizes resilience, determination, and unwavering dedication to excellence. Since my early childhood, I have been immersed in the vibrant tapestry of my family's legacy, a history molded by the remarkable individuals who came before me.

Allow me to introduce myself; I am Marie Antonette Waite, a proactive figure in the realms of branding, public speaking, and entrepreneurship. With extensive experience across diverse industries and a fervent commitment to empowering individuals and businesses, I strive to bring a unique perspective to every project. Through my work, I aim to inspire, educate, and empower audiences, enabling them to elevate their brands, amplify their voices, and make a lasting impact in their respective industries.

At the heart of my family's story is my grandfather, Latino Gonzalez, a towering figure in the world of martial arts. With his unwavering passion for karate and his steadfast commitment to upholding its traditions, he laid the foundation for our enduring family legacy. From him, we not only inherited a love for martial arts, but also a profound sense of responsibility to carry forward his teachings and values.

My father, Rolando Gonzalez, is the embodiment of the values instilled in him by his father. From an early age, he displayed an innate talent for karate, honing his skills under the guidance of esteemed instructors. But his journey would extend far beyond the confines of the dojo. As a respected member of the police force, he exemplified leadership and dedication to ensuring public safety. His role as a physical director at the Philippines Merchant Marine Academy further evidenced his commitment to physical fitness and discipline, shaping the next generation of maritime professionals. Additionally, within the entertainment industry, he made substantial contributions by infusing his karate expertise into various film projects and concert productions.

Similarly, my uncle, Roberto Gonzalez, left an indelible mark on Philippine cinema. Through his creative vision and passion for storytelling, he contributed to the vibrant arts scene. Together, my father and uncle brought authentic martial arts action to the silver screen, captivating audiences with their dynamic performances and commitment to excellence.

My mother, Patricia Gonzalez, is a trailblazer in her own right. She was the first female black belt in our family and shattered stereotypes while paving the way for other women in martial arts. Her contributions extend far beyond the dojo as well. In the Philippines, she served as the President of the Parent-Teacher Association and worked tirelessly to improve public schools and ensure access to quality education for every child. Her dedication to serving her community and uplifting others is a testament to her unfaltering commitment to making a positive impact on society.

One particular memory stands out in my mind, a poignant reminder of my father's enduring love and support. As I faced uncertainty and apprehension about the future during my graduation, my father stood by my side, providing strength and reassurance. With his guidance and encouragement, I confidently embraced the next chapter of my life. However, this journey was not without its challenges. In the midst of my academic pursuits, I found myself at odds with the college administration after raising my voice against injustices perpetrated by a nun. This led to my dismissal from the college, leaving me disheartened and uncertain about my next steps. That's when my father, Rolando, stepped in. He approached the college authorities and tirelessly fought for my reinstatement, ensuring my right to complete my education. Thanks to his determination, I was granted permission to finish my degree and overcome the obstacles that threatened to derail my dreams.

Even after graduation, the road ahead posed challenges. Despite my qualifications, finding employment proved to be daunting. Once again, my father stepped in to support me. He took it upon himself to advocate for my candidacy, standing outside potential employers' offices every day and ensuring that my skills and talents were recognized. His tireless commitment to my success served as a constant source of motivation, spurring me on even in the face of adversity.

Reflecting on these pivotal moments in my life, I am reminded of the depth of my father's love and the lengths he would go to ensure my happiness and well-being. His selflessness and dedication are a testament to the strength of our bond and reflect the values instilled in me from a young age. As I navigate adulthood, I am grateful for his ongoing guidance, and the support which has shaped me into the person I am today.

Today, people still recognize me by my parents' name. When they realize that I am their daughter, their eyes brim with pride. They are grateful for the love and support my family has given them. It was crucial for me to write this book so that people can learn about the significant aspects of their lives and the contributions they made to society. Everything they did was driven by love and compassion.

By sharing our family's story, this book seeks to honor the contributions of the Gonzalez family and preserve their rich legacy for future generations. It is a testament to their resilience, determination, and unwavering faith in the face of adversity. I invite you, dear reader, to embark on a journey through these pages and discover the Gonzalez family's remarkable legacy. May their story inspire and empower future generations. Through their remarkable achievements and unwavering commitment to excellence, the Gonzalez family has made an indelible mark on Philippine society, inspiring countless individuals to pursue their dreams and make a positive impact on the world.

With deepest gratitude,
Marie Antonette Waite

Introduction to Karate: A Journey Through Time

I magine stepping back in time to the island of Okinawa, a place steeped in tradition and ancient wisdom. Centuries ago, the people of Okinawa found themselves in a unique position, surrounded by powerful neighbors who influenced their culture in unexpected ways. As the winds of history swept across the island, the people of Okinawa developed a remarkable system of self-defense born out of necessity.

Known as karate (which means 'empty hand'), this martial art was not just about fighting, it was a way of life... a philosophy that taught respect, discipline, and harmony with one's surroundings. The roots of karate stretch back to a time when Okinawa was a melting pot of cultures, with influences from China, Japan, and Southeast Asia shaping its identity. From these diverse influences emerged a system of combat that blended striking, grappling, and defensive techniques into a seamless whole. In the early days, karate was passed down through oral tradition, with knowledge transmitted from teacher to student in a sacred bond of trust and respect. Techniques were honed through rigorous practice, with practitioners learning to harness their inner strength and focus their energy with precision.

As the years passed, karate began to spread beyond the shores of Okinawa, carried by travelers, merchants, and warriors who recognized its value. In mainland Japan, karate found fertile ground to take root and flourish, evolving into different styles and schools as it adapted to new environments and cultural influences. In the 20th century, karate underwent a period of rapid transformation, propelled by visionaries like *Gichin Funakoshi* and *Chojun Miyagi* who sought to popularize the art and preserve its essence for future generations. With the advent of modern communication and transportation, karate's reach expanded beyond Japan, crossing oceans and continents to touch the lives of people around the world. Today, karate is practiced by millions of people of all ages and backgrounds, from humble dojos in rural villages to bustling urban centers. It has become more than just a martial art - it is a global phenomenon, a symbol of strength, resilience, and unity.

Karate's journey from ancient Okinawa to the modern world is a testament to its remarkable evolution as both a practical self-defense system and a profound philosophy of life. Originally developed as a means of survival in a turbulent world, karate transcended its martial roots to become a holistic discipline that encompasses physical, mental, and spiritual aspects. At its core, karate is more than just a set of techniques, it is a way of being... a path of self-discovery, and personal growth. Through centuries of practice and refinement, karate practitioners have come to understand that true mastery lies not only in the ability to defend oneself but in the cultivation of inner strength, resilience, and wisdom. Embedded within karate's movements and forms are deep-rooted principles of respect, humility, and harmony with nature, reflecting the cultural and philosophical underpinnings of its Okinawan heritage.

As karate spread to mainland Japan and beyond, it absorbed influences from Zen Buddhism, Confucianism, and other spiritual traditions, enriching its philosophical framework and expanding its reach. Today, karate is practiced by people of all ages and backgrounds, each finding their own meaning and purpose in its teachings. Whether in the dojo or in everyday life, the lessons of karate resonate beyond the physical realm, guiding practitioners on a journey of self-discovery and personal transformation.

At the heart of karate lie a set of timeless principles and values that serve as the bedrock of its practice and philosophy. Discipline, the cornerstone of karate, instills in practitioners the dedication and commitment to strive for continuous improvement, both on and off the dojo floor. With each punch, kick, and block, *karatekas* learn the importance of focus and self-control, harnessing their energy and concentration to overcome obstacles and challenges. Respect is another fundamental tenet of karate ingrained in the very fabric of its traditions. From bowing to one's sensei to showing courtesy towards fellow practitioners, karate teaches us to honor and appreciate the contributions of others, fostering a sense of camaraderie and mutual respect within the dojo community. Humility, too, plays a vital role in the practice of karate, reminding us that true strength lies not in arrogance or bravado, but in humility and modesty.

As we progress along the path of karate, we come to understand that there is always more to learn, more room for growth, and that each setback or failure is an opportunity for introspection and self-improvement. Perseverance, perhaps the most enduring virtue of all, fuels the relentless pursuit of excellence in karate. It is the willingness to push through pain, fatigue, and doubt, to keep going even when the odds seem insurmountable. In the face of adversity, karate teaches us to stand tall, to never give up, and to keep moving forward with unwavering determination. These principles: discipline, respect, humility, and perseverance, are not just abstract ideals; they are the guiding lights that illuminate our path in karate and in life. They remind us that the true essence of karate lies not in the mastery of techniques or the accumulation of trophies but in the cultivation of character, integrity, and resilience.

In the dojo, the principles of discipline, respect, humility, and perseverance are not just abstract concepts;

they are lived and breathed in every moment of karate practice, shaping the character and spirit of practitioners. Discipline manifests itself in the rigorous training regimen of karate, where practitioners must adhere to strict routines and protocols, showing up consistently and putting in the effort required to hone their skills. Through disciplined practice, *karatekas* learn the value of hard work and dedication, laying the foundation for success not only in karate but in all areas of life.

Respect permeates every interaction within the dojo, from bowing to one's sensei and fellow practitioners to treating training partners with kindness and consideration. By showing respect towards others, *karatekas* cultivate a sense of unity and harmony within the dojo community, fostering a supportive and inclusive environment where everyone can thrive. Humility is perhaps most evident in the way *karatekas* approach their training, recognizing that there is always more to learn and that no one is ever truly a master. In the dojo, rank and status fade away, replaced by a shared commitment to growth and self-improvement.

Karate teaches us to embrace failure and setbacks with humility, using them as opportunities for reflection and growth, rather than sources of shame or frustration. Perseverance is the driving force behind every *karateka's* journey, propelling them forward in the face of challenges and adversity. Whether it's mastering a difficult technique, overcoming physical limitations, or persevering through grueling training sessions, *karatekas* learn to push past their limits and discover untapped reservoirs of strength and resilience. In the crucible of the dojo, where sweat and determination are the currency of progress, perseverance becomes more than just a virtue... it becomes a way of life.

Together, these principles of discipline, respect, humility, and perseverance form the foundation upon which personal growth and character development are built. Through the practice of karate, individuals learn not only how to defend themselves but also how to navigate life's challenges with grace, integrity, and resilience.

As we continue our exploration of karate's rich history, we encounter a group of remarkable individuals whose contributions significantly shaped the martial art and its enduring legacy. At the forefront stands Latino H. Gonzalez, a visionary master who was renowned for his expertise in Filipino karate. With a lifelong dedication to karate, Latino seamlessly merged ancestral wisdom with modern innovations, establishing a distinct style rooted in Okinawa *Shorin-ryu*. His emphasis on fluid movements, strategic breathing, and the harmonious balance of hard and soft techniques left an indelible mark on practitioners worldwide.

Roberto Gonzalez also emerged as a charismatic sensei whose passion for karate inspired countless students. Raised in a family steeped in martial arts tradition, Roberto's dynamic teaching style, honed under the guidance of his father, continues to shape the karate community, instilling values of discipline, respect, and perseverance.

Rolando Gonzalez, brother to Roberto, embodied strength and wisdom within the karate community. With a quiet demeanor and commitment to excellence, Rolando set a profound example for aspiring martial artists. His teachings emphasized humility, perseverance, and self-discipline, guiding students on a transformative path of personal growth.

Meanwhile, Patricia Gonzalez, Rolando's wife, played a pivotal role in supporting their dojo and community. As a dedicated practitioner and supportive partner, Patricia's contributions extended beyond the mat, nurturing a vibrant karate community built on mutual respect and camaraderie. Her leadership, passion, and commitment continue to serve as a beacon of inspiration, encouraging practitioners of all genders to pursue their martial arts journey with vigor and determination.

Together, the legacies of Latino H. Gonzalez, Roberto Gonzalez, Rolando Gonzalez, and Patricia Gonzalez have not only shaped the evolution of karate but continue to inspire practitioners worldwide, serving as guiding lights for generations of martial artists. In this book we will uncover the captivating stories and profound legacies of these extraordinary individuals, learning how their legendary dedication, commitment, and boundless love for karate have left an indelible mark on its history and legacy.

In our exploration of karate's vibrant tapestry, it's also imperative to acknowledge the diverse voices and experiences within its global community. From bustling urban hubs to remote villages, practitioners of karate come from varied backgrounds, cultures, and walks of life, enriching the practice with their unique perspectives. In the inclusive realm of karate, everyone finds a welcoming space, regardless of age, gender, or ability, fostering a sense of belonging and camaraderie. This spirit of inclusivity lies at the core of karate, reflecting its universal appeal and accessibility. Furthermore, it's essential to recognize the invaluable contributions of women to karate's history and development.

Despite historical challenges, women have played integral roles as practitioners, instructors, and leaders within the karate community. In the chapters ahead, we also celebrate women in karate, celebrating their achievements, highlighting their contributions, and acknowledging their vital role in shaping the martial art's history and legacy.

Driven by a deep-seated passion for karate, this book aims to share its rich history, philosophy, and practice with a diverse audience, spanning from novices to seasoned enthusiasts. By tracing karate's origins, evolution, and global significance, we gain insight into its cultural influences and multifaceted nature as both a self-defense system and a way of life. We will get to know each of the key figures in the Gonzalez family, offering a comprehensive exploration of their lives, teachings, and impact. Throughout these chapters, fundamental principles such as discipline, respect, humility, and perseverance are emphasized, providing practical guidance for personal growth and character development. We also gain insight by exploring the diverse styles and techniques of karate, enriching our understanding and appreciation of this ancient martial art. Whether seeking to learn the basics or deepen your knowledge, this book will be a valuable companion on your journey through the world of karate, offering inspiration and insight for practitioners at every level.

LATINO H. GONZALEZ
"Father of Philippine Karate"

Chapter 1
Latino Gonzalez

The Origins of Karate:
Tracing Its Roots to Okinawa

*K*arate, the ancient martial art that has captured the imagination of millions around the globe, finds its origins deeply embedded in the rich history and culture of Okinawa, a small island located in the Ryukyu archipelago of Japan. To truly understand karate's essence, one must delve into the historical and cultural context of Okinawa, exploring the unique blend of influences that shaped the development of this dynamic martial art.

Okinawa, historically known as the Ryukyu Kingdom, was a strategic crossroads of trade and cultural exchange between China, Japan, and Southeast Asia. This position exposed Okinawa to various influences, including Chinese martial arts, which significantly contributed to karate's evolution. The practice of martial arts in Okinawa, initially referred to as *'te'* or *'ti'*, can be traced back to the 14th century, where it was primarily observed among the warrior class and royal court.

Karate as we know it today began to take shape during the 17th century, a period marked by political instability and social upheaval in Okinawa. In response to a series of invasions and occupations by foreign powers such as the *Satsuma* clan of Japan and the *Ming* and *Qing* dynasties of China, Okinawan peasants and villagers were forbidden from carrying weapons, leading to the development of unarmed combat techniques as a means of self-defense.

During this tumultuous period, Okinawan martial artists refined their fighting techniques, drawing from a diverse range of influences including indigenous Okinawan martial arts, Chinese kung fu, and Southeast Asian fighting styles. Early forms of karate were characterized by simplicity, efficiency, and practicality; emphasizing strikes, kicks, and blocks designed to quickly and effectively incapacitate opponents. One pivotal figure in the development of Okinawan karate was Sokon Matsumura, a legendary martial artist and military advisor to the Ryukyu Kingdom. Born in 1797, Matsumura was famed for his mastery of the martial arts and his efforts to preserve and disseminate Okinawan fighting techniques. Under his guidance, karate began to take on a more structured and organized form, with the establishment of formal training methods, kata (pre-arranged forms), and dojos (training halls).

Another influential figure in the history of Okinawan karate was Anko Itosu, a student of Sokon Matsumura and a respected educator in Okinawa. Itosu is credited with introducing karate into the Okinawan school system and developed the *Pinan* kata, a series of foundational forms still practiced in many styles of karate today. Through his efforts, karate gained widespread popularity among Okinawan youth and began to spread beyond the shores of Okinawa to mainland Japan and beyond. As karate continued to evolve and spread throughout Okinawa, it became increasingly intertwined with the island's cultural identity, serving as a means of physical fitness, self-discipline, and spiritual development.

Karate masters such as Choshin Chibana, Chojun Miyagi, and Kenwa Mabuni further refined and systematized the art, founding their own schools and styles that would later become known as *Shorin-ryu*, *Goju-ryu*, and *Shotokan*, respectively. Despite its humble origins as a form of self-defense practiced by Okinawan peasants and villagers, karate has become a global phenomenon embraced by people of all ages, genders, and backgrounds. Its journey from Okinawa to the world stage reflects the enduring appeal and universal relevance of this ancient martial art with its roots remain firmly planted in the soil of its birthplace.

The spread of karate beyond Okinawa began in the early 20th century, driven by the efforts of pioneering karate masters and the changing geopolitical landscape of Japan. One of the pivotal moments in karate's history was the introduction of the art to mainland Japan by Gichin Funakoshi, an Okinawan karate master and founder of *Shotokan* karate. In 1922, Funakoshi was invited to demonstrate karate at the First National Athletic Exhibition in Tokyo, which marked the first time karate was showcased to a wider audience in Japan. Impressed by Funakoshi's skill and the effectiveness of karate as a martial art, Japanese martial artists and educators began to take an interest in the art, leading to the establishment of the first karate dojo in mainland Japan. Funakoshi's teachings, rooted in the principles of *Shotokan* karate, emphasized character development, self-discipline, spiritual growth, and physical technique. Many Japanese practitioners resonated with his approach, and karate gained popularity as a form of physical education and self-improvement. During this time, other Okinawan karate masters traveled to mainland Japan to introduce their styles and teachings to a wider audience. Chojun Miyagi, founder of *Goju-ryu* karate, and Kenwa Mabuni, founder of *Shito-ryu* karate, were among the prominent figures who contributed to the spread and development of karate in Japan. Each of these masters brought their unique perspective and techniques to the art, enriching its diversity and appeal.

The popularity of karate continued to grow in Japan throughout the 20th century, fueled by the establishment of karate organizations, competitions, and tournaments. In 1955, the *All Japan Karate-do Federation* (AJKF) was formed, marking a significant milestone in the formalization and standardization of karate as a sport. The AJKF introduced standardized rules and regulations for karate competitions, paving the way for its inclusion in international sporting events like the Asian Games and eventually the Olympic Games. At the same time, karate was spreading beyond Japan to other parts of the world, carried by Japanese immigrants and military personnel stationed abroad. Karate clubs and schools began to spring up in countries such as the United States, Europe, and Latin America, attracting eager practitioners drawn to its physical and mental benefits.

In recent decades, karate has continued to evolve and adapt to the changing needs and interests of practitioners worldwide. While some focus on the traditional aspects of karate, preserving its rich cultural heritage and philosophical teachings, others embrace it as a competitive sport, participating in tournaments and championships at local, national, and international levels. Today, karate enjoys widespread popularity as both a martial art and a sport, with millions of practitioners spanning the globe.

Pioneering Karate in the Philippines

L atino H. Gonzalez, often referred to as the "Father" of karate in the Philippines, holds a significant place in the history of martial arts in the country. His pioneering efforts and dedication to karate played a pivotal role in popularizing the art form and laying the groundwork for its growth and development in the Philippines. Born into a family with a rich tradition of martial arts, Latino Gonzalez inherited a passion for karate from a young age. His journey to mastery began with his early training in various martial arts disciplines, including *Arnis de Mano*, *Filipino Ditso (Ju-jitsu)*, and *Kodokan Judo*. However, it was his encounter with Japanese karate that would shape his destiny and lead him to become a trailblazer in the world of martial arts.

In the mid-1950s, Latino established the first commercial self-defense club in the Philippines, which he named the *Commando Self-Defense Club*. Here, he began teaching his version of *Filipino Ditso* and *Kodokan Judo*, drawing on his diverse background in martial arts. His sons, Rolando and Roberto Gonzalez, both experts in the fighting arts, assisted him in his endeavors, further enriching the training experience for students.

As Latino delved deeper into the world of karate, he recognized the need to refine and enhance his understanding of the art form. He began teaching the

Kyokushin-kai style of Japanese karate but later transitioned to the *Shorin-ryu* style of Okinawan karate. This shift marked a significant turning point in his martial arts journey, as he sought to align himself with a style that resonated more deeply with his philosophy and principles.

To further elevate his practice of Okinawan karate, Latino Gonzalez sought out the expertise of renowned instructors, including Seikichi Iha and Seigi Shiroma, both senior practitioners in the *Miyahira Shorin-ryu Karate Association.* Their guidance and mentorship helped refine Latino's technique and deepen his understanding of the intricacies of *Shorin-ryu* karate. He journey was enriched by frequent visits from Grandmaster Katsuya Miyahira, the head of the *Okinawa Shorin-ryu Karate Kyokai.* Grandmaster Miyahira's visits provided an opportunity for Latino to showcase the progress of *Shorin-ryu* karate in the Philippines and receive valuable feedback and guidance from one of the foremost authorities in the field. Under Grandmaster Miyahira's leadership, Latino and his sons, Roberto and Rolando, achieved significant milestones in their karate journey.

A Martial Arts Journey of Mastery, Innovation, and Spiritual Enlightenment

*L*atino Gonzalez eventually achieved the rank of 9th Degree Black Belt, a testament to his mastery and expertise in *Shorin-ryu* karate. Meanwhile, Roberto and Rolando were promoted to 7th Degree Black Belt, acknowledging their dedication and contributions to the art form.

As Latino retired from administrative duties, he entrusted the leadership of karate to his sons, Roberto and Rolando Gonzalez, who continued to uphold and spread the traditions of Okinawan *Shorin-ryu* karate in the Philippines. Following in his father's footsteps, Roberto authored a book titled *"Karate Complete,"* further solidifying the family's legacy in the world of karate. The book focused on *Shorin-ryu* karate and served as a valuable resource for practitioners seeking to deepen their understanding of the art form and its techniques. Today, *Shorin-ryu* remains a popular and respected style in the country, thanks in large part to the pioneering efforts of Latino and his family. His legacy continues to inspire generations of martial artists in the Philippines and beyond, serving as a shining example for aspiring practitioners and reminding them of the transformative power of karate as both a physical discipline and a way of life.

Latino's journey to mastery was driven by a relentless pursuit of excellence and a commitment to pushing the boundaries of his own abilities. His early exposure to various martial arts disciplines laid the foundation for his eclectic approach to training and teaching karate. By incorporating elements from *Arnis de Mano*, *Filipino Ditso*, *Kodokan Judo*, and Japanese karate, he developed a comprehensive and holistic understanding of martial arts principles and techniques. From his early days as a practitioner, he recognized that true martial arts excellence transcends the mere repetition of movements; it requires a connection with one's inner self, a blending of mind, body, and spirit. As he honed his skills and rose through the ranks, Latino imbued each technique with intention, mindfulness, and a profound sense of purpose. Whether executing a *kata*, practicing *kumite*, or teaching a class, he approached each moment with focus and presence, instilling in his students a reverence for the art form and a deep appreciation for its transformative potential.

Through dedicated practice and introspection, practitioners could confront their fears, overcome their limitations, and unlock new levels of confidence and self-assurance. Latino viewed karate as a form of personal growth, a path towards becoming the best version of oneself. He encouraged his students to set goals, challenge themselves, and persevere in the face of adversity. By pushing past their comfort zones and embracing the journey of mastery, practitioners could develop resilience, discipline, and a growth mindset that extended far beyond the dojo.

Latino also emphasized the importance of creative expression in karate. He believed that each individual brought a unique perspective and energy to their practice, and that karate offered a canvas for self-expression and exploration. By encouraging students to infuse their techniques with passion, spirit, and authenticity, he empowered them to unleash their creativity and tap into their innermost emotions and experiences. Through self-discovery, personal growth, and creative expression, Latino sought to inspire his students to live with purpose, authenticity, and vitality. Latino's passing marked the end of an era in Philippine karate, but his legacy lives on through the continued practice and propagation of *Shorin-ryu* karate in the country.

Karate Icons: Yamaguchi & Gonzalez's Transformative Collaboration

*I*n the annals of karate history, the collaboration between Gogen Yamaguchi and Latino H. Gonzalez stands out as a testament to the power of cross-cultural exchange and a shared passion for the martial arts. Yamaguchi, renowned as the "Cat" for his agility and speed, was the founding father of *Goju-ryu* karate, a style characterized by its harmonious blend of hard and soft techniques. Their meeting of minds and spirits marked the beginning of a transformative journey that would leave an indelible mark on the world of karate. Their partnership was forged at a time when karate was still in its nascent stages in the Philippines. Latino, already esteemed for his expertise in Okinawan *Shorin-ryu* karate, recognized in Yamaguchi a kindred spirit; a fellow innovator committed to advancing the art of karate and propagating its virtues globally. Under Yamaguchi's tutelage, he underwent a profound evolution, integrating elements of *Goju-ryu* into his own teaching methodology. The result was a unique synthesis of techniques and philosophies that enriched the karate landscape in the Philippines and beyond. Both Yamaguchi and Latino shared a profound reverence for the spiritual dimensions of karate; a belief that true mastery of the martial arts transcends mere physical prowess. For them, karate was not merely a means of self-defense but a path to self-discovery, self-discipline, and self-realization. Their teachings emphasized the importance of inner harmony, mental fortitude, and spiritual growth; a legacy that continues to inspire practitioners to this day.

Moreover, their collaboration facilitated cultural exchange and understanding between Japan and the Philippines. Through their partnership, they bridged the gap between Eastern and Western martial arts traditions, fostering mutual respect and admiration among practitioners on both sides of the Pacific. Theirs was a partnership built on a shared commitment to excellence, innovation, and the preservation of karate's rich heritage.

The legacy of Gogen Yamaguchi and Latino H. Gonzalez endures through the generations of karate practitioners who have been inspired by their teachings and example. Their collaborative efforts paved the way for a new era of karate instruction, characterized by innovation, inclusivity, and a deep reverence for tradition. As we honor their memory and celebrate their contributions to the world of martial arts, let us remember the enduring spirit of cooperation and friendship that defined their partnership; a testament to the transformative power of karate to unite people across cultures and continents in a shared pursuit of excellence and harmony.

Blending Traditions, Inspiring Generations

*L*atino's Gonzalez's transition from Okinawan karate to the development of his own unique style in the Philippines marked a significant chapter in the global spread and evolution of karate. Born out of a deep respect for the traditional martial arts of Okinawa and a desire to adapt them to the cultural context of the Philippines, his journey exemplifies the dynamic nature of karate as it transcends geographical boundaries and embraces diverse influences.

Emphasizing fluid movements and strategic breathing techniques, Latino created a harmonious balance of hard and soft techniques. His approach reflected a synthesis of traditional Okinawan principles with Filipino martial arts and other influences. This fusion of styles resulted in a dynamic and versatile form of karate that resonated with practitioners in the Philippines and beyond.

One of the key aspects of Latino's impact on the evolution of karate beyond Okinawa and Japan was his role in the formation of the *Philippine Amateur Karate Association* (PAKA) in 1958. Through PAKA, he sought to promote the practice and development of karate in the Philippines, establishing a platform for collaboration, education, and competition. Under his leadership, PAKA became instrumental in organizing karate events, training seminars, and belt promotions, thereby facilitating the growth and recognition of karate as a legitimate martial art in the Philippines.

Today, Latino Gonzalez's legacy lives on through his students and disciples, who continue to propagate his teachings and philosophy around the world. His impact can be seen in the myriad karate schools and organizations that bear his influence, as well as in the countless practitioners who have been inspired by his example. His enduring influence extends beyond the realm of karate, encompassing broader themes of personal empowerment, cultural exchange, and global collaboration. By bridging the gap between Eastern and Western martial arts traditions, Latino helped foster greater understanding and appreciation for the diversity of martial arts practices worldwide. Through his technical innovations, philosophical insights, and inclusive approach to practice, he has left an indelible mark on the martial arts community, inspiring practitioners to strive for excellence and innovation in their own karate journeys.

"Karate is not for the faint of heart. It requires dedication, discipline, and unwavering determination to succeed."
- Miyamoto Musashi

Conclusion

In tracing the journey of karate from its roots in Okinawa to its global spread, we encounter inspiring figures like Latino H. Gonzalez, whose pioneering spirit and dedication to the art have left an indelible mark on martial arts history. Latino's journey exemplified the dynamic evolution of karate, blending traditional Okinawan principles with influences from Filipino martial arts and beyond. Through his leadership in forming organizations like the *Philippine Amateur Karate Association* (PAKA) and his innovative teaching methodologies, he propelled karate into the mainstream, inspiring countless practitioners worldwide. His legacy extends far beyond the confines of the dojo, embodying themes of personal empowerment, cultural exchange, and global collaboration. As we reflect on Latino's contributions, let us remember the transformative power of karate to unite people across cultures and continents in a shared pursuit of excellence and harmony.

Chapter 2
Roberto Gonzalez

Inspiring Mastery
Through Martial Arts Wisdom

*I*n the world of martial arts, the bond between a father and son can be particularly strong, especially when both share a deep passion for karate. Such is the case with Latino and Roberto Gonzalez, a dynamic father-son duo whose influence reverberates throughout the karate community. Latino H. Gonzalez, widely regarded as the "Father" of karate in the Philippines, laid the foundation for Roberto's martial arts journey. As a master of Philippine karate, Latino's dedication to the study and practice of karate served as a source of inspiration for his son from an early age. Growing up in a household where karate was not just a hobby but a way of life, Roberto was immersed in the rich traditions and teachings of his father.

Roberto's upbringing in a family deeply entrenched in martial arts tradition provided him with a solid foundation for his own journey as a karate master. From a young age, he was exposed to the principles of discipline, respect, and perseverance that are fundamental to the practice of karate. Roberto learned not only the physical techniques of karate but also the importance of mental fortitude and spiritual growth.

The influence of Latino H. Gonzalez on Roberto's martial arts journey cannot be overstated. Latino's wisdom, expertise, and dedication to the art of karate served as a guiding light for Roberto as he embarked on his own path as a martial artist. From his father, Roberto inherited not only a love for karate but also a sense of duty to uphold and preserve its traditions. As Roberto's father and mentor, Latino instilled in him a deep appreciation for the history and philosophy of karate, emphasizing the importance of humility, perseverance, and self-discipline. Through his own example, Latino taught Roberto the value of hard work and dedication in achieving mastery in the martial arts.

As Roberto progressed in his training, he began to carve out his own path as a karate practitioner, blending traditional techniques with modern training methodologies. Inspired by his father's teachings and his own experiences on the mat, Roberto developed a dynamic teaching style that resonated with students of all ages and backgrounds. Throughout his journey, Roberto remained committed to upholding the values instilled in him by his father. His dedication to his craft served as an inspiration to aspiring practitioners around the world, demonstrating the transformative power of karate to shape both body and mind. Roberto's impact on the karate community extends far beyond the walls of the dojo. As a charismatic sensei with a genuine passion for karate, Roberto inspired countless individuals to embark on their own martial arts journey.

Through his dynamic teaching style and infectious enthusiasm, Roberto created a supportive and inclusive environment where students of all ages and abilities could thrive. His dedication to sharing the art of karate with others helped foster a sense of camaraderie and mutual respect within the karate community. With influence reaching beyond his immediate circle of students, he actively contributed to the promotion and growth of karate on a broader scale. Through his involvement in karate organizations and events, Roberto played a vital role in raising awareness of the martial art and its benefits.

"The mediocre teacher tells.
The good teacher explains.
The superior teacher demonstrates.
The great teacher inspires."
- William Arthur Ward

Throughout his career, Roberto remained committed to upholding the core principles of karate. These values not only shaped his personal journey but also influenced the lives of countless students privileged to train under his guidance. Through his tireless efforts to promote karate and instill its values in others, Roberto inspired generations of practitioners to strive for excellence and innovation. As his martial arts journey progressed it became one of self-discovery and personal growth as he expanded his knowledge of various martial arts disciplines. His diverse experiences in both karate and film provided him with a unique perspective on the art of combat, shaping his teaching philosophy in profound ways.

"Success is not final, failure is not fatal:
It is the courage to continue that counts."
- Winston Churchill

Drawing upon his own experiences as a student and practitioner, Roberto sought to inspire and empower his students to achieve their full potential both on and off the mat. Throughout his career, Roberto's teaching philosophy was characterized by a combination of traditional techniques and modern training methodologies. He emphasized the significance of discipline, respect, and perseverance, instilling these values in his students as they navigated their own martial arts path. Roberto's growth as a martial artist and his evolution into a dynamic sensei demonstrated his profound commitment to the art of karate and his enduring passion for spreading its transformative power to others.

A Martial Arts Maestro and Cinematic Legend

R oberto Gonzalez's journey was shaped by a diverse range of experiences, including his venture into the world of film. Those experiences played a significant role in shaping his teaching philosophy and approach to martial arts instruction. His involvement in the film industry provided him with a unique platform to showcase his martial arts skills and share his passion for karate with a wider audience. Through his roles in various films, Roberto not only honed his physical prowess but also gained valuable insights into the art of combat and the principles of discipline and perseverance. The intersection of martial arts and film allowed him to explore different facets of his identity as both a martial artist and an entertainer. His experiences on the movie set taught him the importance of discipline, focus, and adaptability, qualities that he would later incorporate into his teaching philosophy.

Roberto encouraged his students to embrace challenges, push past their limitations, and strive for excellence in everything they do. Through his teachings, he emphasized the importance of staying true to oneself and maintaining a strong sense of integrity, both on and off the mat. He instilled in his students the value of perseverance and resilience, urging them to never give up in the face of adversity. These teachings extended beyond physical techniques; he emphasized the importance of cultivating inner happiness, self-belief, and self-empowerment in his students. This holistic approach to martial arts focused on nurturing the mind, body, and spirit, empowering individuals to unlock their full potential and lead fulfilling lives. One of the central tenets of Roberto's teaching philosophy was the belief that true happiness comes from within. He encouraged his students to cultivate a positive mindset and develop resilience in the face of challenges. Through meditation, visualization, and mindfulness practices, he helped his students cultivate inner peace and serenity, enabling them to navigate life's ups and downs with grace and composure.

Roberto instilled in his students a deep sense of self-belief and confidence. He taught them to trust in their abilities and embrace failure as an opportunity for growth and learning. By fostering a supportive and encouraging environment, he pushed them to overcome self-doubt and insecurity, enabling them to pursue their goals with courage and conviction. In addition to inner happiness and self-belief, he also emphasized the importance of self-empowerment. He taught his students to harness their inner strength and tap into their innate potential to effect positive change in their lives and communities. Through goal-setting, visualization, and action planning, Roberto empowered his students to take ownership of their destinies and create the life they desire.

Karate Chronicles: Taking On Film Production

R oberto's entrepreneurial spirit led him to establish his own movie production company, which played a pivotal role in promoting martial arts through cinema. His decision to start a movie production company stemmed from his passion for both martial arts and filmmaking. Inspired by his own experiences as a martial artist and actor, Roberto recognized the potential of using film to showcase the beauty and effectiveness of karate techniques. With his own company, Roberto gained creative control over his projects, allowing him to authentically portray martial arts on screen. This autonomy enabled him to produce films that not only entertained but also served as educational tools for aspiring martial artists creating a platform to elevate the visibility of martial arts within the entertainment industry. Through his films, Roberto aimed to dispel misconceptions about the martial arts and highlight their profound philosophical principles. This marked a significant milestone in his career, demonstrating his commitment to promoting martial arts on a global scale. Through his innovative approach to filmmaking, Roberto bridged the gap between martial arts and mainstream media, leaving a lasting impact on both industries. He also gained valuable insights into communication, storytelling, and visual representation, which he seamlessly integrated into his role as a martial arts instructor.

One key way in which film production influenced his teaching philosophy was in the realm of visual learning. Recognizing the power of visual cues and demonstrations, Roberto leveraged his filmmaking skills to create instructional videos and visual aids that enhanced the learning experience for his students. By capturing karate techniques on film, he provided his students with a comprehensive visual reference, allowing them to observe and analyze movements with precision and clarity.

Roberto's experiences in film production also sharpened his ability to communicate complex concepts and principles effectively. Making use of his background in storytelling and scriptwriting, he developed engaging and memorable lessons that deeply resonated with his students. Through the use of anecdotes, metaphors, and real-life examples, he conveyed timeless philosophical teachings inherent in the martial arts. His involvement in film production instilled in him a sense of creativity and innovation that was evident in his teaching style. He encouraged his students to think outside the box, experiment with different techniques, and adapt their training to suit their individual strengths and preferences. By fostering a culture of creativity and exploration, he empowered his students to unlock their full potential and discover their own unique paths in karate.

As a prolific figure in Philippine cinema, Roberto made an indelible mark with his impressive body of work spanning over 100 movies. From action-packed thrillers to martial arts epics, his versatility as an actor captivated audiences for decades. Some of his notable films included *Ako ang Lalagot sa Hininga Mo*, *Wala ka Nang Lupang Tatapakan*, and *Heroes Hill*, where he showcased his martial arts prowess and charismatic screen presence. In films like *Karate Showdown* and *Target: Karate King*, he demonstrated his mastery of karate, captivating viewers with his dynamic fight scenes. His portrayals of iconic characters like Bertong Ipu-Ipo in *Bertong Ipu-Ipo* and King of the Slums in *Hari ng Slums* further solidified his status as a cinematic legend.

Throughout his career, Roberto fearlessly embraced a diverse range of roles, from noble heroes to cunning villains, displaying his versatility as an actor. In such films as *Basta Bisaya* and *Liquidation Squad*, he portrayed complex characters grappling with moral dilemmas, adding depth and dimension to his performances. His collaborations with renowned filmmakers and fellow actors resulted in some of the most memorable moments in Philippine cinema, earning him accolades and recognition from audiences and critics alike. As a *karateka*, Roberto brought authenticity and intensity to his fight scenes, elevating the martial arts genre to new heights and inspiring generations of aspiring practitioners. Beyond his on-screen achievements, his dedication to his craft and tireless work ethic established him as a respected figure in the film industry.

One of the defining characteristics of Roberto's filmography is its diversity in terms of genre and storytelling. While many of his films revolve around martial arts action, his range as a filmmaker shined through as he explored various themes and narratives, highlighting his versatility and skill as a filmmaker. From action-packed thrillers to heartfelt dramas, Roberto's films captivated audiences with their engaging storylines and dynamic performances, and they often incorporated elements of Filipino culture and heritage, using vibrant cinematography, traditional music, and authentic costumes to celebrate his roots and showcase the rich tapestry of Filipino martial arts traditions.

His films are renowned for their emphasis on moral values and life lessons, reflecting his strong belief in the transformative power of martial arts. Whether depicting the journey of a humble martial artist overcoming adversity or the triumph of good over evil, Roberto's movies left viewers with a sense of hope, resilience, and determination. His filmography also reflected his commitment to promoting positive representations of martial arts and martial artists. Unlike some action films that glorify violence or sensationalize combat, Roberto's work focused on the discipline, honor, and integrity inherent in martial arts practice. Through the actions and choices of his characters, he conveyed important messages about perseverance, self-discipline, and the pursuit of excellence.

Beyond his accomplishments in film, Roberto Gonzalez's contributions to the martial arts community are vast. He served as a practitioner, instructor, filmmaker, and cultural ambassador. Throughout his career, he dedicated himself to promoting the art of karate and empowering individuals to reach their full potential through martial arts practice. As a practitioner, he achieved mastery in various styles of karate, continuously refining his skills through extensive training and experience. His steadfast commitment to excellence and personal growth served as an inspiration to aspiring martial artists, demonstrating the rewards of hard work and passion. Roberto's achievements in tournaments and demonstrations earned him widespread recognition and respect within the martial arts community.

Innovating Karate: Training and Filmmaking

Roberto Gonzalez's innovations in the field of martial arts were characterized by his forward-thinking approach to training, teaching, and promoting karate. Throughout his career, he introduced new techniques, methodologies, and philosophies that revolutionized the practice of karate and inspired practitioners to push the boundaries of their training. From his development of innovative training drills to his pioneering work in martial arts filmmaking, Roberto's contributions had a profound impact on the martial arts landscape.

One such innovation was his development of dynamic training drills designed to enhance speed, power, and agility in karate practitioners. As a competitor and instructor he recognized the need for specialized drills that could simulate the intensity and unpredictability of real-world combat scenarios. In response, he created a series of drills that focus on rapid-fire techniques, footwork, and reaction time, challenging students to think quickly and adapt to changing circumstances. These drills became a cornerstone of Roberto's teaching methodology, helping students develop the skills and instincts necessary to excel in both tournament and self-defense situations.

In addition to his work in training methodology, Roberto also tread new ground in the world of martial arts filmmaking. Combining elements of traditional martial arts choreography with modern cinematography techniques, Roberto has created visually stunning films that capture the essence of karate in action and inspire a new generation of martial arts enthusiasts to explore the art form for themselves.

At the forefront of promoting karate as a holistic practice that encompasses not only physical fitness but also mental and spiritual well-being, his teachings emphasized the importance of cultivating inner strength, self-awareness, and emotional resilience in addition to technical proficiency. He encourages students to develop a mindset of continuous self-improvement and to apply the principles of karate to all areas of their lives. By fostering a culture of personal growth and introspection, Roberto empowered students to become not only skilled martial artists but also compassionate, confident, and resilient individuals.

Conclusion

R oberto Gonzalez's journey as a martial artist and
filmmaker was an inspiring testament to the
transformative power of karate. Through his deep-rooted
passion for the art and his commitment to its principles,
Roberto not only achieved mastery in karate but also
became a dynamic sensei, mentor, and cultural ambassador.
His innovative approach to training, teaching, and
filmmaking revolutionized the martial arts landscape,
inspiring generations of practitioners to push the
boundaries of their own potential. Roberto's dedication to
promoting positive representations of martial arts and
instilling its values of discipline, respect, and perseverance
shone through in both his on-screen performances and his
teachings.

Let's take away from Roberto's story the importance of
embracing challenges, fostering resilience, and striving for
excellence in all aspects of our lives. Whether on the mat or
in the cinema, Roberto Gonzalez's legacy will continue to
inspire and empower individuals to embark on their own
journeys of self-discovery and personal growth through the
practice of karate.

KARATE
COMPLETE

BY
ROBERTO A. GONZALEZ

Chapter 3
Rolando Gonzalez

An Icon of Dedication and Influence

R olando Gonzalez, a towering figure in the world of karate, was renowned for his mastery of Okinawan karate and his multifaceted career beyond the dojo. Born and raised in the Philippines, Rolando's journey into martial arts began at a young age, influenced by his family's deep-rooted tradition in karate. With a lineage tracing back to his father, Latino H. Gonzalez, known as "The Father of Filipino Karate," Rolando inherited a passion for martial arts and a commitment to excellence. Under the guidance of his father and other esteemed instructors, Rolando honed his skills and developed a profound understanding of karate's principles. In addition to his martial arts prowess, Rolando embarked on a diverse career path that encompassed law enforcement, education, and the entertainment industry.

A Multifaceted Legacy:
Martial Arts and Beyond

As a respected member of the police force, Rolando demonstrated leadership and dedication in maintaining public safety. His role as a physical director at the Philippines Merchant Marine Academy showcased his commitment to fitness and discipline, shaping the next generation of maritime professionals. He also made significant contributions to the entertainment industry, particularly in film production and concert promotion. Collaborating with his brother Roberto, a prominent figure in Philippine cinema, Rolando infused his karate expertise into various film projects, bringing authentic martial arts action to the silver screen. His involvement in concert production also highlighted his versatility and entrepreneurial spirit, further solidifying his impact beyond the realm of karate. Throughout his illustrious career, Rolando exemplified the values of perseverance, integrity, and compassion, leaving an indelible mark on the karate community and society at large.

Rolando trained under esteemed instructors in Okinawan karate, including influential masters who imparted invaluable wisdom and techniques. Through their guidance, he deepened his understanding of karate's traditional roots and refined his skills to become a formidable martial artist in his own right. Rolando's martial arts lineage not only reflects a rich heritage of karate mastery but also underscores the importance of passing down knowledge and expertise from one generation to the next.

Beyond his role as a martial artist, Rolando Gonzalez's career encompassed a diverse range of roles and responsibilities, reflecting his multifaceted talents and interests. As a lieutenant stationed at the Philippine Port Authority Police, he served as a physical director, instilling discipline and physical fitness among his fellow officers. His leadership and expertise in martial arts were instrumental in training law enforcement personnel in self-defense techniques and enhancing their overall readiness for duty. He also made significant contributions to the field of education as the Physical Training Director at the Philippines Merchant Marine Academy. In this role, he shared his knowledge of physical fitness and martial arts with cadets, helping to instill discipline, resilience, and a sense of responsibility among future maritime professionals.

Rolando also had a strong presence in the entertainment industry and cultural promotion. He showcased his martial arts skills in films with his brother Roberto, bringing karate to a wider audience and captivating viewers with their dynamic performances. In the world of concert production, he provided a platform for showcasing Filipino talent and cultural heritage, enriching the vibrant arts scene in the

Philippines. Throughout his multifaceted career, Rolando exemplified dedication, versatility, and a commitment to excellence in every endeavor he pursued. His contributions to law enforcement, education, entertainment, and cultural promotion underscored his wide-reaching impact, leaving a lasting legacy in multiple spheres of society.

As a respected martial arts instructor, Rolando's impact on his students transcended the physical techniques of karate, instilling in them valuable life lessons of discipline, perseverance, and self-confidence. Many of his students credited Rolando's guidance and mentorship for their personal and professional success, recognizing him not only as a teacher, but also as a role model and source of inspiration. Rolando's commitment to community service and philanthropy made a lasting impression on those he supported throughout the years. Known for his kind-heartedness and willingness to lend a helping hand, Rolando touched the lives of countless individuals through his charitable endeavors and acts of compassion. Whether assisting those in need or encouraging aspiring martial artists, his generosity and compassion left an indelible mark on his community and beyond. His legacy as a cultural ambassador and promoter of Filipino heritage was evident in his efforts to showcase the rich traditions of the Philippines through martial arts demonstrations, cultural events, and artistic performances. By preserving and celebrating Filipino culture, Rolando contributed to a greater appreciation and understanding of the country's diverse heritage, both domestically and internationally.

Martial Arts Maestro
on the Silver Screen

A s an actor, Rolando appeared in numerous films, captivating audiences with his dynamic performances and martial arts prowess. His presence on the screen brought authenticity and depth to his roles, earning him acclaim and recognition from fans and critics alike. Whether he was portraying a seasoned martial artist, a law enforcement officer, or a charismatic leader, Rolando's on-screen charisma and versatility captivated audiences and solidified his status as a respected figure in Philippine cinema.

Throughout the 1970s and 1980s, Rolando was an established part of Philippine cinema with memorable performances in films like *King of the Dragon* (1974), *Tagisan ng lakas* (1974), and *Kaaway na mortal* (1973). In the film *Hari ng Ninja* (1969), he portrayed a formidable ninja warrior, showcasing his martial arts prowess on the silver screen. His versatility as an actor was evident in diverse roles, from action-packed dramas to thrilling adventures. This also includes appearances in iconic Filipino films such as *Chinatown: Sa kuko ng dragon* (1988), *Estibador* (1980), and *Kodengo Penal: The Valderama Case* (1980). His talent and dedication to his craft also landed him roles in action-packed films like

Napoleon Agra (1978), *Malabanan* (1978), and *Asawa ko silang lahat* (1977).

His commitment to authenticity and dedication to his craft earned him recognition as a skilled martial artist and actor. Rolando's performances served as a testament to his passion for storytelling and his desire to uplift his community through the power of cinema. His contributions behind the scenes as a martial artist and actor were equally significant and he played a pivotal role in shaping the narrative and aesthetics of the films he starred in while influencing Philippine cinema.

Martial Artist Mentor and Community Champion

In addition to his remarkable achievements in martial arts and the film industry, Rolando Gonzalez also made significant contributions to the Tondo community in Manila, Philippines. Despite not being a native of Tondo, he felt a deep sense of responsibility towards the residents of this vibrant neighborhood, recognizing the challenges they faced and the need for positive change. As a witness to the struggles of Tondo's residents with crime and social injustice, Rolando took it upon himself to lend a helping hand, spearheading various initiatives aimed at enhancing the safety and well-being of the community. He worked tirelessly to address issues such as poverty, education, and crime prevention.

Through his leadership and advocacy, Rolando rallied the support of fellow community members and local authorities, fostering a spirit of unity and collaboration in the pursuit of common goals. He organized neighborhood watch programs, youth development initiatives, and educational campaigns to empower residents and create a safer, more prosperous environment for all. These efforts did not go unnoticed. The people of Tondo embraced him as one of their own, recognizing his unwavering commitment to their welfare. In gratitude for his selfless dedication and tireless advocacy, Rolando earned the esteemed title of the "King of Tondo," a symbol of respect and admiration from the community he served. Despite the challenges and obstacles he faced, Rolando remained steadfast in his commitment to making a positive difference in the lives of Tondo's residents. His legacy of compassion, leadership, and service continues to inspire future generations to work towards a brighter, more inclusive future for all.

Behind Rolando Gonzalez's public persona as a martial artist, instructor, and community leader was a rich personal life filled with love, family, and meaningful connections. Despite a busy schedule and numerous responsibilities, Rolando remained deeply committed to his family, cherishing the time spent with loved ones and nurturing strong bonds that transcend martial arts and professional endeavors. At the heart of Rolando's personal life was his relationship with his wife and children. As a devoted husband and father, he prioritized family time and actively participates in shared activities, celebrations, and milestones. His supportive presence and unwavering love provided a source of strength and encouragement for his family members, fostering a warm and nurturing home environment where everyone felt valued and supported.

A Fatherly Figure of Wisdom and Compassion

Rolando's unwavering support for me, his daughter, demonstrated his generous and compassionate nature. He went above and beyond to ensure my well-being and success, leaving no stone unturned in his efforts to assist me. When I faced obstacles on my educational journey and was unjustly blocked from graduating college for speaking out against injustices, Rolando stepped in. He advocated for my rights to the college administration and ensured that I could graduate with peace of mind. On another occasion when I was struggling with a particular employment opportunity, Rolando recognized my predicament and sprang into action. He personally approached the company owner, highlighting my achievements and advocating for my employment. His dedication was unmatched. This unwavering commitment ensured that the employer understood the value of hiring me and helped to secure my first job, serving as a beacon of inspiration.

Rolando was respected and admired wherever he went, whether at restaurants or among friends and family. His calm demeanor and innate dignity earned him reverence from those around him. When Rolando celebrated his birthday, the entire community was always invited. The street was closed off as people gather to join him in a grand birthday celebration. Rolando's popularity was evident in the way people greeted him - their body language revealed their respect as they bowed their heads when saying hello. He was truly loved by many.

Once, at a cheerful gathering, an unexpected incident disrupted the joyful atmosphere, causing a shift in mood and rising tensions. Rolando, in the midst of the laughter and warm conversations, became the unfortunate target of a bottle that struck him, resulting in a stunned silence and shattered glass. Blood trickled down his forehead, staining his face, abruptly ending the lighthearted gathering. However, despite the chaos unfolding around him, Rolando managed to remain remarkably composed. With a calm and steady demeanor, he skillfully prevented the situation from escalating any further. In that moment of turmoil, Rolando's poise and decisive actions showcased his inner strength and resilience. His ability to maintain composure in the face of adversity exemplified true grace under pressure. Thanks to Rolando's presence of mind, the unexpected turn of events did not spiral out of control, preserving the peace and harmony of the gathering.

Martial Arts Philosopher and Spiritual Guide

R olando Gonzalez's teachings about inner self-power and calmness were deeply rooted in the principles of traditional martial arts philosophy, emphasizing the importance of mental strength, emotional resilience, and spiritual harmony. Through his years of practice and instruction, Rolando imparted valuable lessons to his students on how to cultivate inner strength and find peace amidst life's challenges.

Central to Rolando's teachings was the concept of mindfulness, which involves being fully present in the moment and aware of one's thoughts, feelings, and surroundings. By practicing mindfulness techniques such as deep breathing and visualization, students learned to quiet the mind, reduce stress, and cultivate a sense of inner calmness.

Rolando instilled in his students the belief that they possess the power to overcome any obstacle or adversity through sheer determination, perseverance, and self-belief.

By cultivating a strong sense of self-confidence and self-efficacy, students were better equipped to face life's challenges with courage and conviction.

Another thing that Rolando emphasized in his teaching was the correct utilization of power due to proper positioning of the body. This technique delivers more power than muscles alone can. Similarly, he taught his students how to kick with quickness and maintain strong balance on the ground. Stance plays a significant role in karate, and Rolando taught his students to ensure their entire body was centered and balanced when performing techniques. Furthermore, Rolando emphasized the importance of having a positive mindset and treating oneself and others with kindness. He taught his students to feel good about themselves and show compassion and acceptance towards themselves and others, and to understand that true strength comes from within, promoting inner peace and harmony. Through these teachings, Rolando helped his students build confidence, courage, and conviction to face life's challenges with strength, determination, grace, and integrity.

Rolando encouraged his students to approach their training with an open heart and mind, embracing the journey of self-discovery and growth with humility and appreciation. He taught not only physical techniques but also broader principles of ethical behavior, moral values, and spiritual enlightenment. Living by example, he treated people from all walks of life with great respect and kindness, extending a helping hand to those in need, and showing generosity and compassion towards all.

As we reflect on the remarkable journey of Rolando Gonzalez, it becomes evident that his legacy transcends the boundaries of time and space, leaving an indelible mark on the world of martial arts and beyond. His dedication, unparalleled skill, and profound impact on countless lives cemented his status as a legendary figure in the karate community and a beacon of inspiration for generations to come.

Rolando's legacy is defined not only by his achievements in martial arts but also by the values he embodied and the principles he upheld. Throughout his illustrious career, he exemplified the highest standards of discipline, integrity, and humility, serving as a role model for aspiring martial artists and leaders alike.

His teachings emphasized the importance of perseverance, self-discipline, and respect, instilling in his students a sense of purpose and direction that extended far beyond the confines of the dojo. His enduring influence reached into the broader martial arts landscape, where his contributions continue to shape the practice and philosophy of karate worldwide.

Through his innovative techniques, dynamic teaching methods, and commitment to excellence, he inspired countless practitioners to push their boundaries and strive for greatness in all aspects of their lives. His legacy lives on through the countless students and disciples who carry forth his teachings, ensuring that his impact will be felt for generations to come.

Beyond his contributions to martial arts, Rolando's legacy is also evident in the dedication he had to community service, mentorship, and philanthropy. Throughout his life, he remained deeply committed to giving back to his community and supporting those in need, embodying the spirit of compassion and generosity that defined his character. Whether through his work with law enforcement agencies, educational institutions, or charitable organizations, Rolando continued to make a positive impact on the lives of others, leaving a legacy of kindness, compassion, and service.

"The purpose of human life is to serve and to show compassion and the will to help others."
- Albert Schweitzer

Conclusion:

R olando Gonzalez's journey was a testament to the power of dedication, perseverance, and passion. From his early days training in karate to his multifaceted career spanning law enforcement, education, and entertainment, Rolando's impact was profound and far-reaching. His legacy extended beyond the realm of martial arts, touching the lives of countless individuals through his teachings, mentorship, and acts of kindness. As we reflect on Rolando's remarkable journey, we are reminded of the importance of striving for excellence, embracing diversity, and making a positive difference in the lives of others. Rolando Gonzalez's legacy will continue to inspire future generations to pursue their dreams with courage, integrity, and compassion, ensuring that his impact on the world will endure for years to come.

Chapter 4
Patricia Gonzalez

Inspiration for Generations

*P*atricia Gonzalez, the beloved matriarch of the Gonzalez family, was born and raised in a humble home in the Philippines. From a young age, she developed a strong interest in physical activities and martial arts. Despite the societal norms and expectations for women during that time, Patricia was determined to pursue her passion. Her upbringing instilled in her a deep sense of resilience, compassion, and determination, shaping her character and guiding her journey in life.

As Patricia matured, her commitment to personal growth and empowerment led her to explore various avenues for learning and self-discovery, setting the stage for an extraordinary future. Throughout her formative years, Patricia's experiences and challenges fueled a desire to break barriers and defy expectations. Despite facing skepticism and resistance, she remained undeterred, demonstrating remarkable determination to carve out a path in the martial arts world. With steadfast determination and a thirst for knowledge, her journey of self-discovery and empowerment laid a foundation for future accomplishments and contributions to the martial arts community.

As a woman aspiring to excel in karate Patricia encountered numerous challenges and obstacles, but she refused to let any barriers hinder her progress. She remained focused on her goal of achieving mastery in karate and proving that gender should not limit one's potential in martial arts. Her journey was marked by countless hours of training, dedication, and perseverance. She approached each training session with determination and discipline, pushing herself beyond her limits to refine her skills. Despite moments of doubt, Patricia remained focused, never losing sight of the black belt that would symbolized her martial arts mastery. She holds the remarkable title of being the first female black belt in her field, a testament to the power of determination and perseverance in the world of martial arts.

Holistic Wellness Expert and Compassionate Caregiver

*P*atricia Gonzalez is a master of alternative therapies, using a wide range of techniques to promote holistic wellness and healing. As a skilled massage therapist, she tailors her methods to address each client's unique needs.

Swedish massage, with its long, flowing strokes, helps relax muscles, improve circulation, and relieve tension. Deep tissue massage on the other hand targets deeper layers of muscle and connective tissue, providing relief from chronic pain and stiffness. Patricia's expertise in myofascial release techniques enables her to release restrictions in the fascia, improving mobility and reducing discomfort. She also incorporates aromatherapy into her sessions, harnessing the therapeutic benefits of essential oils for relaxation and emotional well-being.

Patricia's journey toward helping others feel better took an interesting turn when she worked for the large company *Shiseido*. Recognizing her special qualities, they sent her to Japan for two years to master cosmetology and reflexology. During her time there, she also learned about *Shiatsu* massage and other related skills. She even had the chance to visit *Yamaguchi*, where she pursued her passion for karate. Patricia became incredibly skilled in the beauty industry, and today she utilizes all of her experience and skills to support her family and help her clients.

In reflexology, Patricia applies her knowledge of stimulating reflex points on the feet, hands, and ears to facilitate healing and restore balance to the body. Manipulating these reflex areas helps alleviate tension, improve circulation, and enhance the body's natural healing mechanisms. *Shiatsu* massage involves finger pressure and stretching techniques along the body's meridians, promoting the flow of energy, relieving stress, and enhancing overall vitality. Through acupressure, Patricia applies firm pressure to specific points on the body to alleviate pain, reduce inflammation, and restore harmony to the body's systems. Her background in physical therapy allows her to design comprehensive rehabilitation programs for individuals recovering from injuries or surgeries. She helps her clients regain strength, flexibility, and function, guiding them toward recovery and optimal physical well-being. With her multifaceted approach to alternative therapies, Patricia serves as a compassionate healer and caregiver, dedicated to enhancing the health and wellness of her community.

Her impact extends far beyond the confines of her therapy room. Patricia is a compassionate advocate for holistic wellness who actively engages with her community, offering her expertise and support to individuals seeking to improve their health and quality of life. Through educational workshops, seminars, and outreach programs, she empowers others with valuable knowledge and tools for self-care and personal growth. In her caregiver role, Patricia consistently demonstrates unwavering compassion and empathy toward those in need. Whether she is assisting elderly individuals with mobility issues, providing comfort to patients undergoing treatment for chronic conditions, or offering support to individuals navigating emotional challenges, she approaches each interaction with sensitivity and genuine concern.

One of Patricia's strengths is her ability to create a safe and nurturing environment, fostering trust and openness. Her commitment to community wellness also extends to her involvement in charitable initiatives and philanthropic endeavors. Whether she is volunteering her time at local shelters, organizing fundraising events for medical research, or contributing to community health programs, she actively seeks opportunities to make a positive impact on the lives of others. Her selfless dedication to serving those in need exemplifies the true spirit of compassion and altruism.

Not only does Patricia excel in her professional role, but she also fulfills her responsibilities within her own family. She provides unwavering love, support, and guidance to her children and loved ones. As a nurturing mother and devoted wife, she creates a warm and loving home environment where individuals feel valued, accepted, and cherished. Patricia's ability to balance her professional commitments with her responsibilities as a caregiver reflects her remarkable strength, resilience, and dedication to her family's well-being.

Supportive Partner and Loving Mother

*P*atricia plays a fundamental role in her husband Rolando's martial arts journey; she's the cornerstone of his success and personal growth. As his life partner and confidante, Patricia embodies dedication and love. Her belief in Rolando acts as a constant source of motivation, fueling his passion and commitment to karate. Through her ubiquitous presence and support, Patricia provides a solid foundation for Rolando to thrive, both on and off the mat. Her tireless efforts behind the scenes ensure that he can focus entirely on his training and teaching responsibilities without worrying about logistical or administrative concerns. Moreover, Patricia's keen insight and gentle guidance help Rolando navigate the challenges inherent in the martial arts journey, providing him with invaluable perspective and wisdom. Together, they form a formidable team, united in their pursuit of excellence and dedicated to nurturing a vibrant karate community.

Imagine a scene of serenity and warmth, where two souls, each possessing their own unique beauty, come together in a dance of fate and destiny. Rolando, with his striking charm and undeniable allure, and Patricia radiating joy and grace, captivating hearts with her infectious smile. Their paths crossed one fateful day at the Latino Gonzalez Karate Academy, a place pulsating with energy and determination. As Rolando trained diligently, his gaze fell upon Patricia, whose presence lit up the room like a beacon of light. Sensing a shift in the air, Rolando, ever the gentleman, donned his shirt in a gesture of respect and admiration. Little did they know, this seemingly ordinary encounter would blossom into something extraordinary, weaving a tapestry of love and companionship that would stand the test of time. With courage and determination, Rolando took the bold step of expressing his feelings to Patricia's mother, declaring his intention to make Patricia his life partner. And so, their journey began, a tale of two souls entwined in a bond forged by destiny itself. Through their union, they brought solace and joy to countless lives, their selfless acts of kindness resonating through the fabric of their community. Their love story serves as a reminder that true beauty lies not only in outward appearances but also in the depth of one's character and the purity of their intentions.

Patricia's unwavering support not only strengthens Rolando's resolve but also serves as a beacon of inspiration for students and fellow practitioners, highlighting the transformative power of love, dedication, and partnership in the martial arts journey. Together, they create a nurturing environment where students of all ages and backgrounds can learn and grow, not just as martial artists but also as individuals. Patricia's warmth and hospitality welcome newcomers with open arms, instantly putting them at ease and fostering a sense of belonging. Her genuine care and concern for each student's well-being extend beyond the dojo walls, creating a supportive network that extends into every aspect of their lives. Meanwhile, Rolando's expertise as a martial artist and instructor provides the backbone of the dojo's training program, offering students rigorous instruction combined with compassion and encouragement. His dedication to imparting not just physical skills but also core values such as discipline, respect, and perseverance ensures that students emerge from each class not only stronger but also more resilient and self-confident. Together, Rolando and Patricia form a dynamic duo, complementing each other's strengths and weaknesses to create a dojo environment that is both welcoming and challenging. Their partnership serves as a shining example of the transformative power of martial arts, inspiring students to push beyond their limits and strive for excellence in all areas of their lives.

Patricia and Rolando are not only partners in life but also perfect dance partners, especially when it comes to swing dancing. Their synchronized movements and effortless grace on the dance floor are a sight to behold. They showcased their exceptional dancing skills at their daughter Marie's wedding in 1995, filling the room with joy and celebration. Even after Rolando's passing, Patricia continued to dance, keeping their love for dancing alive. What's amusing is that sometimes she infuses her karate moves into her dancing, adding a unique flair that never fails to entertain. The love and connection they share shines through not only in their martial arts practice but also in their shared passion for dance, reminding us all that love knows no bounds and can be expressed in the most delightful and unexpected ways.

Did you know that when the film industry was searching for a female lead for karate films, Patricia was on the brink of a remarkable chapter in her life? It was during this time that she found herself expecting a child, which unfortunately meant she couldn't seize the opportunity. The role eventually went to Magna Gonzales, who was hailed as the Queen of Karate films. However, Patricia's influence in the world of karate was far-reaching and profound. Despite missing out on the chance to star in films, she played a pivotal role in promoting karate. Through her captivating demonstrations and her father-in-law's karate club, Patricia's impact resonated deeply within the karate community, earning her the title of the true Queen of Karate.

Martial Arts Gaurdian

One sunny afternoon Patricia was out and about, unaware that her trip would soon take a dangerous turn. She boarded the bus and settled into her seat, enjoying the scenic views passing by. However, her peaceful ride was abruptly interrupted when an unruly individual with a masked face attempted to take advantage of her vulnerability. With her heart racing and adrenaline surging, Patricia relied on her years of martial arts training to defend herself. Channeling her inner strength, she reacted swiftly, delivering a powerful elbow strike. The assailant, struggling to breathe and in pain, fell to the ground. Patricia remained composed and took charge of the situation, ensuring the safety of herself and her fellow passengers by escorting the attacker off the bus.

As the dust settled and the bus resumed its journey, Patricia's actions served as a powerful reminder of the importance of remaining vigilant and prepared in the face of unexpected threats. Her bravery and determination exemplified the spirit of martial arts, reinforcing the idea that strength comes not only from physical prowess but also from inner resilience and self-assurance. With renewed confidence, Patricia continued her journey, knowing that she possessed the skills and mindset to overcome any obstacles. Her experiences on the bus underscored the significance of self-defense training and served as a testament to her strong resolve in the face of adversity.

In another alarming moment, Patricia faced a would-be thief who tried to snatch her purse. Without hesitation, she unleashed a swift and precise front kick, thwarting the thief's efforts and knocking him to the ground. The thief, lying on the floor in disbelief, couldn't comprehend how this woman had brought him down with such instinctive moves. This exemplified the essence of karate – quick movements driven by instinct. Throughout both encounters, Patricia's quick thinking and decisive actions ensured her safety, highlighting Patricia's ability to rely on her martial arts skills and resourcefulness to defend herself effectively.

Culinary Maven and Community Pillar

*I*n the heart of their humble abode, Patricia's culinary prowess knew no bounds. Each day, she embarked on a culinary adventure, transforming the kitchen into a haven of aromatic delights and savory flavors. From hearty stews that warmed the soul to wholesome dishes that delighted the senses, Patricia's culinary creations were a labor of love for her family. With skillful hands and a generous heart, she crafted meals that nourished not only their bodies but also their spirits.

For Patricia, cooking was more than just a chore; it was a means of expressing her love and devotion to her family. In the hustle and bustle of daily life, Patricia's cooking became a source of comfort and stability for her loved ones. Whether it was a hearty breakfast to start the day off right or a comforting dinner to unwind after a long day's work, Patricia's meals were a constant reminder of the love that bound their family together. With each bite, they tasted not only the flavors of her culinary creations but also the warmth of her affection. Yet, Patricia's culinary talents extended far beyond the confines of their home. She generously shared her cooking skills by teaching many of her relatives and household assistants, passing down her knowledge and passion for cooking to future generations. Through her guidance, others learned to appreciate the joy of preparing and sharing meals with loved ones, carrying on Patricia's legacy of culinary excellence and familial love.

As a pillar of their community, she generously shared her culinary gifts with friends and neighbors, brightening their days with homemade treats and delicious dishes. Whether it was a dessert for a school fundraiser or cooking a meal for a neighbor in need, Patricia's kindness knew no bounds. Through her culinary creations, Patricia brought joy, comfort, and nourishment to all who crossed her path, leaving an indelible mark on the hearts of those fortunate enough to taste her cooking. Her kitchen was not just a place of culinary creativity but also a sanctuary of love and warmth, where family and friends gathered to share in the simple pleasures of good food and cherished company.

Community Advocate and Testament to Resilience

As the President of the Parent-Teacher Association (PTA) in the Philippines, Patricia worked tirelessly to enhance public schools, ensuring that students received the best education possible. Her leadership and advocacy were instrumental in implementing various initiatives aimed at improving school facilities, curriculum, and resources. However, her commitment to education went beyond administrative duties.

When natural disasters struck and schools were damaged by floods, Patricia didn't hesitate to roll up her sleeves and get involved. She rallied the community together, reaching out to the highest officials to mobilize resources and support for rebuilding efforts. Patricia's hands-on approach and determination played a crucial role in the successful reconstruction of schools, ensuring that students could return to a safe and conducive learning environment. Amidst the challenges, she also took on the responsibility of speaking in public and presenting at municipal and city official meetings. Her aim was to encourage and inspire people to come together and improve the educational facilities in their community. Through her compelling speeches, she ignited a sense of hope and determination among the residents, galvanizing them to take action for the betterment of their schools and the future of their children.

Patricia also made it a priority to visit and support sick friends and acquaintances, offering them comfort and companionship during their most challenging times. Whether it was sitting by their bedside, lending a listening ear, or providing words of encouragement, Patricia's presence brought solace and hope to those in need.

When she came to the US, Patricia faced a new set of challenges, including restrictions on using her physical therapy license. Undeterred, she decided to further her education and became a Certified Nursing Assistant. In this role, she cared for many elderly clients with various health conditions, including Alzheimer's, dementia, and scoliosis. Drawing from her background in physical therapy, Patricia applied her skills to help improve their mobility and quality of life.

Her compassionate approach went beyond basic care; she went the extra mile to brighten their days by dressing them up beautifully and taking them to places that evoked happy memories. Her thoughtful gestures left a lasting impact on her clients, some of whom expressed their gratitude through generous gifts and offers of higher pay just to have her stay longer. Patricia's dedication and love were evident in every interaction, and she became deeply cherished by all those she served. Moreover, Patricia's resilience and strength were evident in her willingness to step up and support her family during difficult times. When her husband faced financial struggles, Patricia took on additional work, dedicating long hours to serving high-end customers to help support her family financially. Her selflessness and determination to provide for her loved ones served as an inspiration to those around her, demonstrating her firm commitment to her family's well-being.

In the tapestry of life, Patricia's story shines as a beacon of courage and resilience. When faced with the daunting news of a tumor in her eye, instead of succumbing to fear, Patricia chose to stand tall against the shadows of uncertainty. With characteristic determination and a heart full of hope, she embarked on a journey of healing and triumph. Through her inspiring battle with cancer, Patricia's spirit illuminated the path for others, reminding us all that in the face of adversity, it is our inner strength and positivity that guide us towards brighter tomorrows.

Today, Patricia is an active member of a Filipino Community Church, where her faith plays a central role in her life. She attributes all her accomplishments to the blessings from God, recognizing His presence in every aspect of her journey. During challenging times, such as battling COVID-19 and recovering from a car accident, Patricia found strength in her faith and relied on her karate instincts to persevere. Moreover, she utilized her therapy skills to aid in her recovery, demonstrating resilience and determination in the face of adversity.

In all aspects of her life, Patricia Gonzalez exemplifies the values of dedication, compassion, and resilience. Her pioneering achievements in martial arts, coupled with her tireless efforts to improve her community and support her family, make her a role model for generations to come.

Patricia's legacy serves as a reminder that with passion, perseverance, and a compassionate heart, one person can truly make a difference in the lives of others and leave a lasting impact on their community.

Compassionate and Inspirational Role Model

*P*atricia's story is a testament to the power of faith, perseverance, and the invaluable lessons learned from her martial arts training. Her unwavering belief in God and commitment to serving her community serve as an inspiration to all who encounter her story. Patricia's kind-heartedness and compassion radiated from her like a beacon of light, touching the lives of everyone fortunate enough to know her. Her gentle demeanor and genuine concern for others endeared her to all who crossed her path, leaving a lasting impression that transcended mere acquaintance. In the bustling community where Patricia and her family resided, her presence was felt far and wide. Whether it was lending a helping hand to a neighbor in need or offering words of encouragement to a friend facing challenges, Patricia's compassionate spirit knew no bounds. She possessed a rare ability to empathize with others, to truly understand their joys and sorrows, and to offer solace and support in times of need.

One of the most remarkable aspects of Patricia's kindness was its authenticity. Her compassion was not borne out of obligation or expectation but flowed freely from her heart, driven by a genuine desire to make a positive difference in the lives of those around her. Whether it was a warm smile, a listening ear, or a comforting embrace, Patricia's acts of kindness were genuine expressions of her caring nature. Her impact extended beyond the boundaries of her immediate community, reaching even the most marginalized and overlooked members of society. Patricia had a special place in her heart for those who were struggling or disadvantaged, and she dedicated herself to uplifting and empowering them in any way she could.

From volunteering at local schools to organizing community events for the less fortunate, Patricia's compassion knew no bounds. Perhaps most importantly, Patricia's kindness served as a powerful example for her family and friends. Through her actions, she taught them the importance of empathy, generosity, and compassion, instilling in them values that would guide them throughout their lives. Her children, in particular, looked up to her as a role model, learning from her example the profound impact that a single act of kindness could have on the world around them. In times of adversity, Patricia's unwavering compassion served as a source of strength and resilience for those around her. Her ability to see the good in others, even in the face of hardship, inspired hope and optimism in those who were struggling. Whether it was offering words of encouragement to a friend facing a difficult situation or lending a helping hand to a stranger in need, Patricia's kindness had a ripple effect, spreading positivity and warmth wherever it went. In a world often characterized by divisiveness and conflict, Patricia's kindness was a beacon of hope, reminding us all of the transformative power of compassion. Her legacy lives on in the countless lives she touched, the hearts she warmed, and the spirits she uplifted.

Patricia Gonzalez's legacy as a trailblazer for women in martial arts is nothing short of inspiring. In a male-dominated field, she shattered stereotypes and paved the way for future generations of female practitioners to pursue their passion for martial arts fearlessly. Her journey was marked by determination, resilience, and an unwavering commitment to breaking down barriers and challenging the status quo. From an early age, Patricia displayed a natural aptitude for martial arts, demonstrating skill and determination that belied her gender. Despite facing skepticism and resistance from some quarters, she refused to be deterred, forging ahead with her training and honing her abilities with unwavering dedication. Through sheer perseverance and determination, she earned her place as a respected martial artist, earning accolades and recognition for her skill and expertise.

As Patricia's reputation grew, so too did her influence within the martial arts community. She became a role model and mentor for aspiring practitioners, offering guidance, support, and encouragement to those following in her footsteps. Through her example, she showed that determination and passion were key ingredients for success in martial arts, inspiring others to pursue their passions with unwavering dedication.

Her choice to join a group mainly composed of seasoned practitioners was driven by her own thirst for knowledge and excellence. Patricia's commitment to mastering karate, despite the challenges she faced, exemplified the idea of pushing oneself beyond comfort zones and embracing challenges head-on. Her story serves as a reminder that true empowerment comes from within, fueled by a relentless pursuit of personal growth and achievement.

Life, she believed, was about breaking free from the confines of comfort and embracing discomfort as a pathway to growth. Patricia's journey was not about seeking special treatment or recognition; it was about harnessing the power within oneself to overcome obstacles and reach new heights of greatness.

By focusing on the individual's journey and the innate potential within each person, Patricia's story speaks to the universal human experience of striving for excellence. Her legacy is a testament to the transformative power of self-belief, determination, and resilience, inspiring others to embrace their own inner strength and pursue their dreams with unwavering conviction.

Reflecting on Patricia's remarkable journey evokes a profound sense of admiration and inspiration. Her unwavering dedication to her craft, coupled with her compassion and resilience, serves as a timeless example of the transformative power of perseverance and kindness. Patricia's journey is a testament to the human spirit's ability to overcome adversity and thrive in the face of challenges. Throughout her life, Patricia has exemplified the values of integrity, humility, and empathy, inspiring countless individuals to pursue their passions with courage and conviction. Her commitment to breaking down barriers and advocating for gender equality has had a lasting impact on the martial arts community and beyond, challenging outdated stereotypes and paving the way for greater inclusivity and diversity.

Moreover, Patricia's presence in the martial arts community has been nothing short of transformative. Her leadership, wisdom, and unwavering support have helped nurture a thriving community built on mutual respect, camaraderie, and shared passion. By fostering an environment where individuals of all backgrounds and abilities feel welcome and valued, Patricia has created a legacy of inclusivity and acceptance that will endure for generations to come. As we reflect on Patricia's journey, we are reminded of the importance of resilience, compassion, and perseverance in the face of adversity. Her example teaches us that true strength lies not in physical prowess alone but in the courage to stand up for what is right and the compassion to uplift others along the way. Patricia's legacy serves as a guiding light for all who seek to make a positive difference in the world, reminding us that our actions, no matter how small, have the power to create lasting change. Patricia Gonzalez's impact on the martial arts community and beyond is immeasurable. Her journey is a testament to the transformative power of resilience, compassion, and dedication, inspiring individuals around the world to pursue their dreams with courage and conviction. As we honor her legacy, let us carry forward the lessons learned from her example, striving to create a world where all are valued, respected, and empowered to reach their full potential.

"I don't run away from a challenge because I am afraid. Instead, I run toward it because the only way to escape fear is to trample it beneath your feet."

- Nadia Comaneci

Conclusion:

Patricia Gonzalez's journey from a humble upbringing in the Philippines to becoming a trailblazer in martial arts and a pillar of her community is a story of resilience, compassion, and determination. Despite societal expectations, Patricia pursued her passion for martial arts with dedication, breaking barriers and inspiring others along the way. Her legacy extends beyond the dojo and kitchen, touching the lives of countless individuals through her kindness, compassion, and advocacy for equality. Patricia's journey reminds us of the power of perseverance and the importance of standing up for what is right, even in the face of adversity. As we reflect on Patricia's remarkable journey, let us carry forward her spirit of resilience and compassion, striving to create a world where all are valued, respected, and empowered to pursue their dreams. Patricia Gonzalez's impact on the martial arts community and beyond will continue to inspire future generations to reach for greatness and make a positive difference in the world.

"Don't limit yourself. Many people limit themselves to what they think they can do. You can go as far as your mind lets you. What you believe, remember, you can achieve."

– Mary Kay Ash

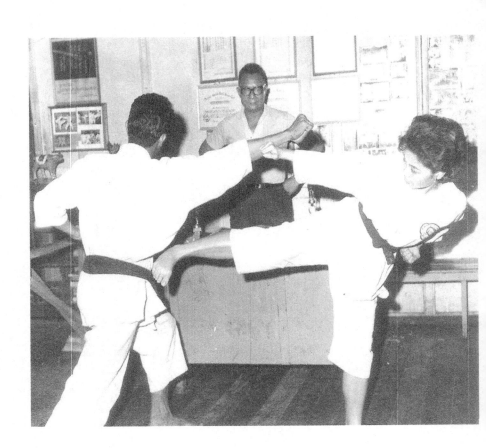

Chapter 5
Online Course
Karate Training

Karate Warm-Up:
A Symphony of Body and Mind

W arming up before karate training is like preparing a canvas before painting a masterpiece. It sets the stage for a safe, effective, and enjoyable practice session. Think of your body as a well-tuned instrument—warm-up exercises fine-tune it, ensuring that it's ready to perform at its best. But why is warming up so crucial? Well, let's break it down. First off, warming up gets your blood pumping and your heart racing. It's like revving the engine of a car before hitting the road. As your heart rate increases, more oxygen-rich blood flows to your muscles, preparing them for action. This increased blood flow also helps loosen up stiff muscles and joints, making your movements smoother and more fluid. But warming up isn't just about getting the blood flowing—it's also about getting your mind in the game.

Think of it as flipping a switch from "off" to "on." Warm-up exercises help shift your focus from whatever you were doing before to the task at hand—karate training. They help clear your mind of distractions and set the stage for intense concentration and focus. They also help rev up your nervous system. Think of your nervous system as the electrical wiring that controls your body's movements. Warm-up exercises help activate this wiring, sending signals from your brain to your muscles more efficiently. This improves coordination, reaction time, and overall motor control, setting the stage for precise and powerful karate techniques. One of the key mental benefits of warm-up exercises is their ability to help focus and center the mind. As you perform each movement with intention and mindfulness during your warm-up, you're bringing your attention to the present moment and cultivating a sense of mental clarity and focus. This focused mindset is invaluable during karate practice, where split-second decisions and precise movements are required.

Moreover, warm-up exercises provide a mental rehearsal for the challenges ahead. As you perform these exercises, you're not just warming up your body—you're also warming up your mind. You're priming your brain for the focus, concentration, and mental toughness required for intense karate training. This mental rehearsal helps sharpen your focus, boost your confidence, and mentally prepare you to tackle any obstacles that may arise during your practice session.Now, let's talk about flexibility. Have you ever tried bending a frozen popsicle stick? Not very flexible, right? Well, cold muscles are a bit like that—stiff and prone to injury. But with a good warm-up, it's like thawing out that popsicle stick. Warm-up exercises gently stretch and lengthen your muscles, making them more flexible and less likely to strain or tear during training. And here's the kicker: warming up can actually help prevent injuries. By gradually increasing the intensity of your movements, warm-up exercises allow your body to adapt to the demands of karate training. This reduces the risk of sudden muscle strains or joint injuries, keeping you safe and injury-free.

So, there you have it—the significance of warming up before karate training. It's like laying down a strong foundation for a house—you wouldn't build without it! Warming up prepares your body and mind, enhances flexibility, and reduces the risk of injuries. It's the secret sauce that makes your karate practice sessions not only safer but also more effective and enjoyable.

In the fast-paced world of karate, injuries are an unfortunate reality. Whether it's a pulled muscle, a sprained joint, or a more serious injury, the risk is always present when engaging in intense physical activity. However, warm-up exercises serve as a powerful tool in mitigating this risk and keeping practitioners safe and injury-free. One of the primary ways warm-up exercises help reduce the risk of injuries is by increasing the elasticity of muscles and tendons. When you perform dynamic stretching exercises during your warm-up, you're not only increasing blood flow to your muscles, but also gently stretching and lengthening the muscle fibers. This improved elasticity allows your muscles and tendons to absorb shock more effectively, reducing the likelihood of strains and tears during karate practice.

Additionally, warm-up exercises help improve joint mobility and range of motion. As you move through a series of dynamic stretches and mobility drills, you're lubricating your joints with synovial fluid and gently mobilizing them through their full range of motion. This helps ensure that your joints are prepared to handle the dynamic movements and sudden changes in direction that are common in karate training, reducing the risk of strains, sprains, and other joint-related injuries. Warm-up exercises help activate and engage the stabilizing muscles around your joints. These smaller, often overlooked muscles play a crucial role in providing support and stability to your joints during movement. By incorporating exercises that target these stabilizing muscles into your warm-up routine, you're strengthening and activating them, which in turn helps prevent imbalances and compensations that can lead to injury.

Neck Exercises in Karate Training

Neck exercises play a pivotal role in the preparation phase of karate training, serving as a crucial component of the warm-up routine. The neck is a central junction connecting the head to the rest of the body, and its flexibility and strength are essential for executing various karate techniques effectively. By incorporating targeted neck exercises into the warm-up regimen, practitioners can enhance their range of motion, improve muscle endurance, and reduce the risk of strain or injury during training sessions. In karate, where precise movements and rapid reflexes are paramount, a strong and flexible neck is particularly advantageous. Whether executing strikes, blocks, or grappling maneuvers, the neck muscles must support the head's movements while maintaining stability and control. Additionally, a well-conditioned neck promotes proper alignment of the spine, which contributes to overall posture and balance.

Moreover, neck exercises stimulate blood flow to the cervical region, promoting nutrient delivery and waste removal from the muscles. This increased circulation helps to alleviate tension and stiffness, allowing practitioners to move more freely and fluidly during training. Furthermore, by engaging in regular neck exercises, karateka can develop greater proprioception – the body's awareness of its position in space – leading to enhanced coordination and kinesthetic sensitivity. Beyond the physical benefits, neck exercises also offer mental and emotional advantages to karate practitioners. As individuals engage in controlled movements and focused breathing during these exercises, they cultivate mindfulness and concentration, essential qualities for effective martial arts practice. Additionally, the sense of empowerment and confidence that comes from mastering challenging neck exercises can have a positive impact on overall self-esteem and mental resilience. Neck exercises form an integral part of the holistic approach to karate training, addressing both the physical and mental aspects of martial arts practice. By incorporating these exercises into the warm-up routine, practitioners can enhance their readiness for training, reduce the risk of injury, and cultivate a deeper connection between mind and body. Now, let's delve deeper into specific neck exercises commonly employed in karate warm-ups, exploring their techniques, benefits, and variations.

Available on our Online Course:

- Techniques and Variations of Neck Exercises
- Precautions and Safety Guidelines for Neck Exercises

Arm Exercises

*I*n the realm of karate, where precise movements and powerful strikes are paramount, the role of the arms cannot be overstated. They serve as the primary tools for executing techniques, whether delivering a devastating punch, executing a swift block, or performing intricate kata sequences. Consequently, ensuring that the arms are properly warmed up and ready for action is of utmost importance in any karate training regimen.

The Arms Exercise segment of the warm-up routine is specifically designed to target and prepare the muscles of the upper body for the rigors of karate practice. This segment encompasses a variety of dynamic movements and stretches that aim to enhance the strength, flexibility, and endurance of the arms, shoulders, and surrounding muscle groups. By engaging in these exercises, practitioners can effectively increase blood flow to the arms, promoting better circulation and oxygenation of the muscles, which is crucial for optimal performance and injury prevention.

Moreover, the Arms Exercise segment serves as a crucial transition from the resting state to the active state, mentally and physically preparing practitioners for the demands of karate training. It serves as a signal to the body that it's time to shift gears, activating the neuromuscular system and priming the muscles for the intense physical exertion that lies ahead. This mental and physical preparation not only enhances performance but also helps reduce the risk of injury by ensuring that the muscles and joints are properly warmed up and lubricated. Incorporating specific arm exercises into the warm-up routine helps improve overall coordination and proprioception, which are essential for executing techniques with precision and control. By engaging in dynamic movements that mimic the actions performed during karate practice, practitioners can enhance their neuromuscular connections and refine their motor skills, leading to more efficient and effective execution of techniques. The Arms Exercise segment is not just about warming up the muscles; it's about priming the entire body for the unique challenges of karate training. It sets the tone for the session ahead, instilling a sense of focus, readiness, and determination in practitioners as they embark on their martial arts journey. So let's explore the specific arm movements and exercises that comprise this vital component of pre-karate warm-ups.

Available on our Online Course:

- Dynamic Arm Movements

Leg Exercise

*I*n the world of karate, the lower body holds immense significance as it forms the basis of technique and movement. Leg strength and flexibility are paramount for practitioners, enabling them to execute techniques with power, precision, and balance. Through focused leg exercises, karateka strive to enhance muscular endurance, facilitating optimal performance during training and competitions alike. Moreover, flexibility in the legs is crucial for expanding the range of motion and fluidity of movement, reducing the risk of strain or injury. By placing emphasis on leg development, practitioners can elevate their performance, unlocking new levels of skill and moving closer to mastery in this ancient martial art. These exercises target key muscle groups such as the quadriceps, hamstrings, calves, and glutes, contributing to improved power generation, speed in kicks, and overall athleticism. By integrating leg exercises into their training routine, martial artists establish a solid foundation for their journey towards mastery in karate.

Chest Exercises in Pre-Karate Warm-Up

*T*he chest plays a crucial role in karate, serving as a central muscle group for executing powerful strikes, blocks, and other techniques. As such, incorporating chest exercises into the pre-karate warm-up routine is essential for preparing the upper body muscles for the physical demands of training. These exercises not only enhance strength and stability but also improve flexibility and range of motion in the shoulders and chest, thereby reducing the risk of injuries during karate practice. One of the primary benefits of including chest exercises in the warm-up is the activation of the pectoral muscles. These muscles are essential for generating power in karate techniques such as punches and blocks. By performing targeted chest exercises before training, practitioners can effectively prime these muscles, allowing for more efficient movement and greater force generation during practice sessions.

Moreover, chest exercises contribute to overall upper body conditioning, which is crucial for maintaining balance and control in karate movements. Strengthening the chest muscles helps support the shoulders and arms, providing a solid foundation for executing various techniques with precision and control. Additionally, these exercises can help improve posture and alignment, reducing the risk of strain or injury during dynamic movements. Incorporating chest exercises into the warm-up also has psychological benefits for karate practitioners. Engaging in focused exercises before training helps mentally prepare individuals for the physical challenges ahead. It allows practitioners to center their attention on their body and breath, promoting a sense of mindfulness and readiness for the training session.

Overall, chest exercises form an integral part of the pre-karate warm-up routine, providing numerous benefits for both physical and mental preparation. By targeting the chest muscles and surrounding areas, these exercises enhance strength, flexibility, and stability, ensuring that practitioners are adequately prepared to perform at their best during karate practice.

Breathing Exercises for Pre-Karate Warm-Up

Breathing exercises play a crucial role in preparing the body and mind for karate training by helping to regulate breathing patterns, increasing oxygen flow to the muscles, and promoting relaxation. Proper breathing techniques are essential for maintaining energy levels, enhancing focus, and improving overall performance during karate practice.

"If you don't do what's best for your body, you're the one who comes up on the short end."
- Julius Erving

Conclusion:

*T*he warm-up segment in karate training is essential for preparing the body and mind for safe and effective practice. Physically, it increases blood flow, flexibility, and muscle readiness, reducing the risk of injury and enhancing performance. Mentally, warm-up exercises promote focus, concentration, and confidence, setting the stage for optimal training sessions. By targeting specific muscle groups such as the neck, arms, legs, and chest, and incorporating breathing exercises, a holistic approach to readiness is ensured. By recognizing the importance of warming up, karate practitioners can maximize their potential, improve their skills, and foster a deeper connection between mind and body. In essence, the warm-up is the cornerstone of successful karate practice, laying the foundation for growth, mastery, and lifelong enjoyment of the martial art.

Chapter 6
Mastering the Basics

Stance

*I*n the journey of mastering karate, understanding the fundamentals is crucial. Among these basics, one of the most essential elements is the stance. Imagine yourself standing confidently, ready to face any challenge that comes your way. This is where the journey begins.

Now, let's delve into the specifics. When we talk about the stance in karate, it's all about balance, stability, and focus. Picture yourself standing sideways, with your weight firmly planted on one foot. This sideways orientation, at a 90-degree angle, allows for optimal mobility and agility in all directions.

But that's not all. The positioning of your other leg is just as important. As you stand, the leg facing forward plays a crucial role. The tip of your foot and your toes should touch the ground, ensuring a solid connection with the surface beneath you. Keep this leg slightly bent, maintaining a sense of readiness and flexibility.

Together, these elements create a foundation of strength and control, essential for executing karate techniques with precision and power. By mastering the stance, you lay the groundwork for further advancement in your karate journey, building confidence and competence with each step forward. So, let's start with the basics and embrace the journey ahead, one stance at a time.

Karate Weapons

*K*arate stands out as a comprehensive fighting system due to its diverse array of "weapons," which extend beyond traditional implements to encompass various parts of the human body. Among these, the fists, feet, elbows, and knees reign supreme for their capacity to deliver powerful strikes while absorbing considerable impact. The efficacy of these weapons relies heavily on proper technique to prevent injury to the practitioner and maximize effectiveness. Moreover, consistent training is necessary to toughen the striking surfaces, ensuring they can withstand the rigors of combat.

Each weapon serves a distinct purpose, targeting specific vulnerabilities in an opponent's defenses. For instance, the more delicate targets like the eyes or temple are best suited for strikes with "weaker" weapons, such as the one-knuckle fist. Conversely, the "strong" weapons like fists and elbows can inflict significant damage on hard or resilient targets with less precision required.

The selection of weapons to employ in a given situation hinges on various factors, including the nature of the target and the practitioner's positioning. Adaptability is key, allowing martial artists to leverage the most effective weapon for the task at hand. However, the mere strength and durability of these weapons are insufficient without proper delivery. Training must emphasize correct form and technique to ensure that strikes are executed effectively in real-world scenarios. This commitment to precision is essential for maximizing the impact of karate's formidable arsenal of weapons.

Mastering the Art of the Punch: Proper Hand Positioning

*I*n the world of karate, the foundation of a powerful punch lies in the proper positioning of the hand. This seemingly simple yet crucial aspect sets the stage for delivering a formidable strike that can make all the difference in combat. Let's delve deeper into the intricacies of hand positioning and explore why it is fundamental to mastering the art of the punch.

Maintaining Shoulder Alignment

When directing your gaze towards the center of your opponent's chest, it's essential to pay close attention to the alignment of your shoulders. Proper shoulder alignment is crucial for generating maximum power and efficiency in your punch while minimizing the risk of injury.

To ensure correct shoulder alignment, start by positioning your shoulders in a relaxed but upright posture. Avoid hunching or rounding your shoulders forward as it can compromise your punching technique and diminish the force behind your strikes. Instead, keep your shoulders squared and level, maintaining a strong and stable foundation for your punch.

As you prepare to unleash your strike, focus on keeping both shoulders parallel to the ground. Avoid allowing one shoulder to drop or rise higher than the other, as it can throw off your balance and impede the effectiveness of your punch. By maintaining equal shoulder height, you optimize the transfer of power from your upper body to your arm, enhancing the force of your punch.

Furthermore, proper shoulder alignment plays a crucial role in protecting against injury during combat. Misaligned shoulders increase the risk of strain or overextension, leaving you vulnerable to sprains, strains, or even dislocations. By consciously aligning your shoulders and distributing the workload evenly between them, you reduce the likelihood of injury and ensure a safer and more effective punching technique.

From a tactical standpoint, maintaining shoulder alignment enhances your overall fighting prowess. Aligned shoulders allow for smoother and more fluid movement, enabling you to transition seamlessly between offensive and defensive maneuvers. Whether launching a devastating punch or evading an opponent's strike, proper shoulder alignment is key to executing martial arts techniques with precision and grace.

Solid Foot Placement

While the upper body generates the force behind a punch, the foundation for this power begins with proper foot positioning. Solid foot placement provides stability, balance, and leverage, allowing you to transfer energy effectively from the ground up through your body and into your strike.

To achieve solid foot placement, start by positioning your feet shoulder-width apart and distribute your weight evenly between them. This balanced stance creates a solid foundation, ensuring stability and preventing you from being easily knocked off balance by counterattacks.Next, focus on grounding both feet firmly into the ground. Imagine rooting your feet into the earth, anchoring yourself like a sturdy tree in a storm. This firm connection with the ground not only enhances stability but also facilitates the transfer of kinetic energy generated by the lower body into the punch.

As you prepare to strike, pay attention to the alignment of your feet. When placing a foot forward, it should be straight from the outside of the foot. This ensures proper alignment and prevents unnecessary strain on the ankle and knee joints. Additionally, ensure that the knee of the forward leg is slightly bent. This slight bend in the knee helps absorb shock and maintain flexibility, allowing for swift and fluid movement during the punch. Moreover, the foot should be positioned slightly more inside to ensure that the outside of the foot is straight. This alignment optimizes stability and prevents the foot from rolling inward or outward, reducing the risk of injury during the punch.

By focusing on these key elements of foot positioning, you can establish a strong and stable foundation for your punches, maximizing power, precision, and efficiency in your strikes.

The foot corresponding to your dominant hand should be positioned slightly behind the other foot, providing a slight rotation of the hips and shoulders that adds power to your punch. Meanwhile, the lead foot should be angled slightly outward, allowing for greater stability and mobility.

Maintaining a solid base with your feet also enables efficient weight transfer during the punch. As you extend your arm forward to strike, shift your weight from the back foot to the front foot, driving your bodyweight into the punch and maximizing its impact. This coordinated movement ensures that the full force of your body is behind the strike, making it more formidable and effective. Additionally, solid foot placement enhances your ability to move dynamically and respond swiftly to changing situations in combat. With a stable foundation, you can pivot, shuffle, or step with precision, adjusting your position to capitalize on openings or evade incoming attacks.

Solid foot placement is essential for maximizing the power, stability, and effectiveness of your punches. By grounding yourself firmly and aligning your feet correctly, you create a strong foundation that allows you to generate and transfer energy efficiently, delivering devastating strikes with confidence and precision. So, remember to establish solid foot placement as you prepare to unleash your punches, and you'll be well-equipped to dominate the battlefield with skill and authority.

Shoulder Movement

In executing a punch, proper shoulder movement plays a crucial role in generating power and ensuring accuracy. The shoulders serve as the conduit through which force is transmitted from the core muscles to the arm, amplifying the impact of the strike.To execute a punch with optimal shoulder movement, begin by maintaining proper alignment and posture. Keep your shoulders relaxed and squared, avoiding any tension or hunching that could impede fluid movement. Imagine drawing your shoulder blades down and back, creating a stable platform from which to launch your attack.

As you initiate the punch, focus on engaging the muscles of the shoulder girdle to drive the movement. Start by retracting the shoulder on the side corresponding to your punching arm, pulling it slightly back and down as you prepare to extend your arm forward. This action primes the shoulder for explosive movement, loading it with potential energy like a coiled spring.

As you extend your arm forward to deliver the punch, maintain the level position of your shoulder to maximize power generation. Avoid lifting or dropping the shoulder during the punch, as this can compromise the integrity of your technique and diminish the force behind the strike. Instead, focus on driving the punch with a powerful rotation of the torso and activation of the core muscles, allowing the shoulder to remain stable and controlled throughout the movement.

Simultaneously, visualize driving energy from your entire body into the punch, harnessing the power generated by your legs, hips, and core muscles. This coordinated effort ensures that the force of the punch is transmitted smoothly through the shoulder and into the target, maximizing impact and effectiveness. As you complete the punch, focus on maintaining balance and stability in your shoulder position. Avoid overextending or hyperextending the shoulder joint, as this can strain the muscles and leave you vulnerable to counterattacks. Instead, aim to deliver the punch with controlled precision, stopping just short of full extension to preserve the integrity of your technique.

Sparring

- Sparring in Karate represents the pinnacle of training, assessing the application of fundamental techniques in simulated combat scenarios.
- It offers a platform to execute techniques against diverse opponents and situations, contributing to skill enhancement and ability refinement.
- Supervision by a competent instructor is imperative to maintain safety standards and ensure proper technique execution.

Benefits of Sparring

- Enables practitioners to assess and refine their skills.
- Provides a platform to develop mental fortitude crucial for combat situations.
- Offers invaluable opportunities for technique enhancement and skill development.

Free-style Sparring

Free-style sparring is characterized by its unscripted nature, where each participant endeavors to land a well-focused punch, kick, or strike while simultaneously defending themselves. This form of sparring provides invaluable training in both mental acuity and physical prowess when facing an opponent. Due to the high level of control required, beginners are advised against participation to avoid potential dangers and the development of undesirable habits.

Key Developments in Free-Style Sparring

1. *Feinting Skills:* Participants learn to employ feints and discern feints from opponents.
2. *Enhanced Observation:* Emphasis is placed on keen observation, minimizing unnecessary movements.
3. *Integration of Limbs:* Utilization of hands and feet in tandem for both defensive and offensive maneuvers is practiced.
4. *Personalized Fighting Style:* Individuals refine techniques tailored to their body size and capabilities.
5. *Versatility in Technique:* Mastery of diverse karate techniques against various types of attacks and attackers is cultivated.

Progression in Sparring Mastery

With dedication to mastering the basics and consistent practice in Free-Style Sparring, individuals gradually transition to instinctive reactions devoid of conscious thought. Unconscious responses represent the pinnacle of sparring proficiency.

Guidelines for Effective Sparring

1. *Seriousness:* Participants are encouraged to approach each sparring session with seriousness, envisioning their partner as a genuine adversary to evoke a cautious and forceful technique execution.

2. *Calmness:* Maintaining a tranquil mindset facilitates accurate assessment of opponent movements, enabling appropriate responses. A composed mind is essential for making sound decisions amidst the intensity of combat, avoiding errors fueled by emotions or distractions.

3. *Honesty in Attack:* It is paramount to approach sparring with honesty, delivering strong and genuine attacks. This approach allows your partner to practice correct defensive responses. A common mistake among beginners is attacking from too far a distance, rendering defense unnecessary. Attacks should be aimed to stop just short of making contact with your partner, ensuring safety while maintaining the integrity of the exercise.

4. *Avoiding Contact:* Under no circumstances should actual strikes be executed on your partner. All attacks must be halted just before reaching their target, prioritizing safety and preventing injury.

5. *Avoid Anticipation:* Refrain from preemptively anticipating your opponent's moves. Wait until the attack is imminent before initiating a block or counterattack. This approach fosters sharper reflexes and enhances the authenticity of the sparring experience.

6. *Maintain Caution:* Remain vigilant and attentive to your opponent's actions throughout the sparring session. Continuous observation facilitates timely responses and minimizes the risk of being caught off guard.

Available On Our Online Course:

Elevate Your Martial Arts Skills with Mastering the Basics

*A*re you ready to take your martial arts journey to the next level? Look no further than our comprehensive online course, where you'll discover a wealth of techniques and forms designed to enhance your skills and deepen your understanding of the martial arts discipline.

Available on our platform, you'll have access to a diverse range of lessons covering essential techniques and forms, including:

- *Punching:* Master six distinct types of punches to sharpen your striking abilities.
- *Elbow Strikes:* Explore five varieties of elbow strikes for close-quarters combat effectiveness.
- *Knife-Hand Strikes:* Learn the art of knife-hand strikes, a versatile and powerful technique.

- *Back-Fist Strikes:* Enhance your arsenal with back-fist strikes, ideal for rapid counterattacks.
- *Kicking:* Refine your kicking prowess with instruction on five different types of kicks.
- *Blocking:* Hone your defensive skills with eight essential blocking techniques to defend against various attacks.
- *Katas:* Immerse yourself in the traditional forms of karate, including *Katas* 1 to 5, *Naihanchin* 1 to 3, *Ping-an* 1 to 5, *Passai-Sho, Passai Dai, Kusangku-Sho, Kusangku Dai, Chinto Gojushiho*, and *Jiong*.

Our course will provide access to all photos with step-by-step instructions, and insightful tips to help you perfect each technique and form. Whether you're a novice seeking to build a strong foundation or an experienced practitioner aiming to refine your skills, our online course offers something for everyone.

Don't miss this opportunity to expand your knowledge and elevate your martial arts journey. Enroll now and embark on a transformative learning experience that will empower you both on and off the mat.

Elevate Your Karate Skills with Free-Style Sparring as a Sport

U nlock the potential of free-style sparring and elevate your karate prowess with our comprehensive online course, "Free-Style Sparring as a Sport." In the realm of martial arts, the evolution of free-style sparring has paved the way for exhilarating karate matches. The success of these competitions hinges not only on highly trained techniques but also on the cultivation of self-control among participants.

Our meticulously crafted course delves into the practical contest rules established by esteemed karate associations worldwide. Through selected excerpts from official regulations, we highlight crucial aspects vital for mastering free-style sparring, including:

- Understanding the essence of free-style sparring and its evolution in karate.
- Exploring the fundamental techniques essential for success in competitive sparring.
- Cultivating an attitude of self-discipline and control crucial for safe and effective sparring.
- Learning the practical contest rules governing free-style sparring, ensuring adherence to standardized regulations.

Whether you're a seasoned practitioner seeking to refine your skills or a novice eager to delve into the world of competitive karate, our online course offers a structured learning experience tailored to your needs.

Join us as we embark on a journey to unlock the full potential of free-style sparring and elevate your karate proficiency to new heights. Enroll now and take the first step towards mastering the art of competitive sparring.

ROBERTO A. GONZALEZ   7TH DAN OKINAWA SHORIN - RYU

入段証

ラティノ H ゴンザレス

右者空手道に精通し
たるを以て 本道場の
審査により 認書の上り
免許す

一九六八年

Latino H. Gonzalez 8th Dan Okinawa 1968

Photostat copy of the Author's grade issued by the Okinawa Shorin-ryu
Karate, 8th Dan.

Okinawa Karate experts with Mr. Gonzalez
when he was in Okinawa — 1967.

Chochin Chibana 10th
Dan Head of Okinawa
Karate Okinawa.

References

1. Washimekai Karate International. Historical background. https://washimekaikarateinternational.weebly.com/historical-background.html

2. History of Okinawa Karate. https://karatedo.hakuakai-matsubushidojo.com/history.html#:~:text=Karate%20(%E7%A9%BA%E6%89%8B)is%20a%20martial,techniques%20such%20as%20knife%2Dhands

3. The Founder of Modern Karate Do. https://web.iyte.edu.tr/~gokhankiper/Karate/Funakoshi.htm#:~:text=If%20there%20is%20one%20man,world%20until%20he%20was%2053

4. The Real Mr Miyagi – Founder of Goju-Ryu. https://www.historyoffighting.com/the-real-mr-miyagi.php#google_vignette

5. What Are the Origins of Karate? https://premiermartialarts.com/blog/what-are-the-origins-of-karate/

6. International Ryukyu Karate Research Society/琉球唐手術國際研究會. https://irkrs.blogspot.com/

7. The Art of Karate. https://oishya.com/journal/the-art-of-karate-a-journey-of-discipline-strength-and-tradition/

8. The Role of Discipline and Respect in Martial Arts. https://truebalancekarate.com/the-role-of-discipline-and-respect-in-martial-arts/

9. History of Karate-do. https://safetyfirst1f1213.blogspot.com/2012/10/history-of-karate-do.html

10. Okinawa Shorin-ryu Clan Philippines Karate Club (1975). http://www.osc.faithweb.com/index.htm

11. Wuko & AD. https://wukophdotnet.wordpress.com/2015/09/28/founders-history/

12. Kamikaze Web. https://www.kamikazeweb.com/showimage.php?text=f&id=02628

13. History of Okinawa Karate. https://www.hakuakaikarate.org/history

14. Karate: A Call for Change. https://appliedshotokan.com/karate-call-for-change/

15. Okinawan Karate Masters - Martial Talk. https://www.martialtalk.com/threads/okinawan-karate-masters.21953/

16. Engaging National Identities: The Arnisador and the Samurai. https://pjssh.upv.edu.ph/wp-content/uploads/2022/01/25-72-89-PJSSH-20-19-20-P01_Engaging-national-identities.-Gonzales-R..pdf

17. Dynamic Life-Style of Shorin-Ryu Inc. https://dynamicircle.wordpress.com/9-4-reblog/

18. Filipino Martial Arts And the Construction of Filipino National Identity. https://research.manchester.ac.uk/files/54566917/FULL_TEXT.PDF

19. Vintage Profile of Karate Great Gogen Yamaguchi. http://cookdingskitchen.blogspot.com/2022/07/vintage-profile-of-karate-great-gogen.html

20. Black Belt Feb 1968. https://books.google.com.pk/books?id=aM4DAAAAMBAJ&pg=PA14&lpg=PA14&dq=The+Roberto+Gonzalez+karate&source=bl&ots=AcW-Go5ksn&sig=ACfU3U1HhK74I3E99kazGor7lnRQ004YAg&hl=en&sa=X&ved=2ahUKEwjXgbP8ot6HAxUjR_EDHbA3Jt0Q6AF6BAg

YEAM#v=onepage&q=The%20Roberto%20Gonzalez%20karate&f=
false

21. Roberto Gonzales Biography. https://movie-
industry.blogspot.com/2007/11/roberto-gonzales.html

22. Roberto Gonzalez (1942-2009). https://www.imdb.com/name/
nm1045418/

23. Tars Tarkas.NET. https://tarstarkas.net/

24. Rolando Gonzales. https://www.imdb.com/name/nm1045419/

25. Essential Karate Techniques for Beginners. https://
www.amaf.com.au/karate-techniques-for-beginners/

Made in the USA
Monee, IL
03 October 2024

67010890R00075